Dr Helen Likierman i̶s̶ a̶ ... ̶ical Psychologist with many years of exp ... and children of all ages. Her ... lping children with emotional, socia ... es, but she also has a long-standing interes ... learning difficulties. Her research work included stu ... pre-school children's social play and friendships. She is also the school counsellor at a large co-educational school and the mother of two teenage children.

Dr Valerie Muter is a Consultant Clinical Psychologist with a wide range of experience working with young children's learning, emotional and behaviour problems. Her work at Great Ormond Street Hospital for Children centres on assessing the needs of children with neurological problems. She also holds Honorary Research Fellowships at the Institute of Child Health and at the Centre for Reading and Language, University of York.

TOP TIPS FOR STARTING SCHOOL

**DR HELEN LIKIERMAN
AND DR VALERIE MUTER**

Vermilion
LONDON

1 3 5 7 9 10 8 6 4 2

Published in 2008 by Vermilion, an imprint of Ebury Publishing

Ebury Publishing is a Random House Group company

Text and illustrations on page 167 © Dr Helen Likierman and Dr Valerie Muter 2006, 2008
Illustrations on page 30 © Nicola Smee 2006

The Random House Group Limited Reg. No. 954009

Addresses for companies within the Random House Group can be found at
www.rbooks.co.uk

A CIP catalogue record for this book is available from the British Library

Mixed Sources
Product group from well-managed
forests and other controlled sources
www.fsc.org Cert no. TT-COC-2139
© 1996 Forest Stewardship Council

The Random House Group Limited supports The Forest Stewardship
Council (FSC), the leading international forest certification organisation. All our
titles that are printed on Greenpeace approved FSC certified paper carry the FSC logo.
Our paper procurement policy can be found at www.rbooks.co.uk/environment

Printed and bound in the UK by
CPI Mackays, Chatham ME5 8TD

ISBN 9780091924133

Copies are available at special rates for bulk orders.
Contact the sales development team on 020 7840 8487 for more information.

To buy books by your favourite authors and register for offers, visit www.rbooks.co.uk

Contents

Acknowledgements

We are grateful to our editor, Julia Kellaway, who has been so enthusiastic about this project and helped us in every possible way.

Helen's husband, Julian Hale, gave huge amounts of time and skill to both commenting on and typing the manuscript. We are enormously indebted to him.

Finally, thanks to Dr Richard Lansdown, Dr Orlee Udwin, Professor Margaret Snowling, Dr Maria Callias, Professor Charles Hulme, Professor Sir Michael Rutter, Professor Faraneh Vargha-Khadem, Professor Brian Butterworth and Dr Angela Morgan – and to David Chamberlain and Nicola Smee for their illustrations.

Introduction

Starting school is a key event in everybody's life. Our aim in *Top Tips for Starting School* is to help smooth the way and make the transition happy and successful.

When children start school, teachers build on skills that have already (they hope!) been put in place during these important pre-school years – language, concentration, behaviour, early reading/writing/number work, becoming independent, getting on well with others and making friends. Does your child have all these skills? Fill in the questionnaires in Chapter 1 to help you find out. Your answers will show you how far your child has already come and what more he or she might do with some active help and encouragement.

Use our hundreds of practical tips and suggestions to help prepare your child for every aspect of school life. Don't worry – these can be easily fitted into your busy day-to-day lives. By making the best use of the time you already spend with your child, you will have more fun together and spend less time dealing with worries or difficulties.

You want your child to be confident, relaxed and eager to learn, ready for school – and life beyond. Let our Top Tips be your guide.

You will notice that your child is referred to as 'he' or 'she' in alternating chapters. The use of a particular gender in no way implies that the chapter is more relevant to one gender than the other.

1

How Ready for School is Your Child?

Overleaf is a short questionnaire for you to complete. It will give you a flavour of some of the specific skills that will be covered in the chapters to come. Of course, you shouldn't expect your child to have mastered all these skills as yet. He is likely to be better at some than others.

Check to see how far you feel your child has come already. Your answers will help you decide how much further you need to go in preparing your child for school.

Do you think your child is able to:	Yes	To some extent	No	Don't know
Self-care				
Manage by himself in the toilet?	☐	☐	☐	☐
Cope with undressing and dressing by himself?	☐	☐	☐	☐
Cope with mealtimes without adult help?	☐	☐	☐	☐
Say his name, address and age?	☐	☐	☐	☐
Behaviour				
Do (mostly) what he is told?	☐	☐	☐	☐
Control (usually) frustration and temper?	☐	☐	☐	☐
Stop himself distracting/interfering with others?	☐	☐	☐	☐
Understand and keep to rules or boundaries?	☐	☐	☐	☐
Social				
Play readily with other children?	☐	☐	☐	☐
Take turns in play?	☐	☐	☐	☐
Agree to share toys and materials?	☐	☐	☐	☐

	Yes	To some extent	No	Don't know
Emotions				
Deal with new situations?	☐	☐	☐	☐
Deal with changes in routine?	☐	☐	☐	☐
Separate happily from parent or carer?	☐	☐	☐	☐
Not cry over slight problems?	☐	☐	☐	☐
Attention/concentration				
Listen to and follow adults' instructions?	☐	☐	☐	☐
Finish a given activity lasting five to 10 minutes?	☐	☐	☐	☐
Stay in a designated area, such as a mat or seat at story or meal times, for 10 to 15 minutes?	☐	☐	☐	☐
Spoken language				
Speak clearly so he is understandable to others?	☐	☐	☐	☐
Understand three-or-four idea sentences (such as 'Put the pink cup on the chair')?	☐	☐	☐	☐
Produce complete sentences of five to six words?	☐	☐	☐	☐

	Yes	To some extent	No	Don't know
Repeat a sentence of eight to 10 words?	☐	☐	☐	☐

Reading

	Yes	To some extent	No	Don't know
Recognise about half of the letters of the alphabet?	☐	☐	☐	☐
Blend (join) two or three sounds to make a word (such as c-a-t makes cat)?	☐	☐	☐	☐
Break spoken words up into syllables (such as pen-cil)?	☐	☐	☐	☐

Numbers

	Yes	To some extent	No	Don't know
Understand comparative size (such as bigger/smaller, most/least)?	☐	☐	☐	☐
Recognise and label simple shapes (such as circles, squares)?	☐	☐	☐	☐
Match objects (such as colours, simple shapes, pictures)?	☐	☐	☐	☐
Count objects up to 10?	☐	☐	☐	☐

Writing	Yes	To some extent	No	Don't know
Control a pencil adequately?	☐	☐	☐	☐
Copy lines (vertical/horizontal), circles and crosses?	☐	☐	☐	☐
Form some letters and numbers recognisably?	☐	☐	☐	☐
Write his first name?	☐	☐	☐	☐

You may find that many of these skills are already in place, or that your child finds some skills easy, but others need more preparation in order to be ready for school. You may also discover that you were not so aware of the importance of some skills.

Some points to keep in mind:

1. Children are Not All Alike

Children vary in how fast their skills develop. For example, some are walking as early as 12 months (or even before), while others are not on their feet until around 18 months. Some children about to start school are not going to be as mature or as ready for formal learning as others.

In addition, within any one child, different skills may develop at different rates. At any given point in time, each child will have an individual pattern of what he is good at and what he is not so good at.

To develop each skill, start at your child's level and build up from there. Your child will learn and develop at his own pace and will pick up some skills faster than others.

2. Boys and Girls are Different

- Girls develop language skills faster. For example, they show quicker vocabulary growth initially, though boys catch up from the age of two.
- Girls have a larger language region of the brain than boys (a biological advantage). But it has also been shown that mothers often talk more to their toddler girls than to their toddler boys (an environmental advantage) so girls have more language practice early on.

- Girls are ahead of boys in reading.
- In school, boys are greater 'risk takers' and end up with more cuts and bruises, whilst girls tend to be more cautious.
- Girls in general try harder than boys to please and to avoid failure.
- Developmental problems are much more common among boys. Speech and language disorders, reading difficulties, attention and overactivity problems, emotional and social immaturity, and naughty and aggressive behaviour are seen in three to five times as many boys as girls.

But let's put these differences into perspective. Over the total population of girls and boys, there are more similarities than differences and any differences are small.

3. Preparing for Starting School is Not Hothousing

Some people believe that providing their children with lots of enriching learning experiences will bring great returns. Preparing your child for school is not about increasing his IQ or making him into a rocket scientist by the time he is 10. Rather, it is about making sure he starts school confidently and is able to deal with the social, educational, practical and behavioural demands of the classroom and playground. This means preparing your child emotionally and socially as well as intellectually and educationally.

⭐ **TOP TIP:** Remember that children have hugely different energy levels, interests, abilities and speeds of development. Have the confidence to do what you feel is right for you and your child, even if it's different from what your friends or neighbours are doing. Also, children need opportunities for free play and self-discovery – and time to just 'chill out'.

2
Develop Language

Acquiring spoken language has to stand out as the most amazing feat of pre-school development. Note that we have said 'acquiring', not learning, language. Parents don't teach their children to understand and use language like teachers teach the alphabet and eventually reading and spelling. Readiness to acquire language is built into our genes and our brains.

To acquire vocabulary and the rules of grammar, children have to hear and imitate language. This means that you and those around your child have a vital role to play in shaping and supporting development of speech and language.

How Children's Language Varies

Young children acquire speech and language at different times. Some 16-month-olds can *understand* 250 words but others of the same age only 100. Similarly, some 16-month-olds may be able to *say* over 100 different words, but others may use only two or three words.

There are things you can look for which will help you separate out normal variation (which isn't anything to worry about) from what may be a language difficulty.

- Although not all children say words by 18 months, most will understand a large number by this age. A good starting point is to look at the number of words your child understands. If she understands a lot of words but is saying little, this is probably not much to worry about. If she seems to understand very few words, this is a cause for concern.

- Another clue as to whether or not a child is having problems with language is to look at the relative number of 'object' to 'action' words she uses; pre-schoolers seem to be able to build up their vocabulary much more quickly if they use lots of object words like 'daddy', 'dog', 'cup' than if they use mainly action words like 'go', 'more'. So if your child is going round naming lots of objects, there probably isn't too much to worry about.

Remember that girls are usually slightly ahead of boys in their initial vocabulary development. After the age of two, boys start to catch up. These gender differences are small and lessen as children get closer to school age.

How Ready for School is Your Child's Language?

The best time to fill in the following questionnaire is when your child is turning four years of age.

Speech and Language Questionnaire

1. Speech

Is your child's speech understandable to you and other family members?

Almost all the time ☐

Most of the time ☐

Some of the time ☐

Almost never ☐

Is your child's speech understandable to people who don't know her well?

Almost all the time ☐

Most of the time ☐

Some of the time ☐

Almost never ☐

Is your child able to produce most single sounds (such as s, t, m) correctly in her everyday speech?

Almost all the time ☐

Most of the time ☐

Some of the time ☐

Almost never ☐

Is your child able to produce most sound 'clusters' (such as /st/ as in 'stone', /fl/ as in 'flower', /th/ as in 'thing', /sh/ as in 'shoe') correctly?

Almost all the time ☐

Most of the time ☐

Some of the time	☐
Almost never	☐

If you've ticked 'almost all the time' or 'most of the time' to these questions, your child's speech seems to be developing quite nicely.

If you've ticked 'some of the time' or 'almost never', it may be that your child's speech sound (known as phonological) development is delayed. You may be able to understand your child's speech (because you're used to it), but if people who don't know her well can't understand what she's saying, this can cause a lot of difficulties and frustrations for her. This in turn could be problematic when she starts school.

2. Vocabulary
How large is your child's spoken vocabulary?

Thousands of words – I've lost count!	☐
Between 500 and 1,000 words	☐
A couple of hundred words	☐
Less than a hundred words	☐

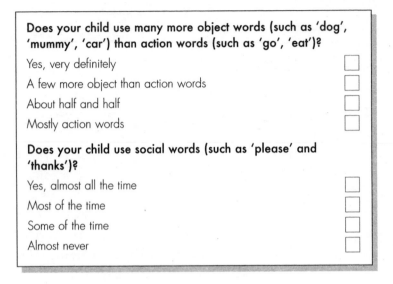

Does your child use many more object words (such as 'dog', 'mummy', 'car') than action words (such as 'go', 'eat')?

Yes, very definitely ☐

A few more object than action words ☐

About half and half ☐

Mostly action words ☐

Does your child use social words (such as 'please' and 'thanks')?

Yes, almost all the time ☐

Most of the time ☐

Some of the time ☐

Almost never ☐

If your child has a large vocabulary that makes use of lots of object words (but brings in other sorts of words as well), she is well on the way to good language development.

If she has a small vocabulary, uses the same few words over and over again and sometimes incorrectly, this could be an indication of a language difficulty.

3. Grammar

Does your child produce sentences of at least five to six words in length (such as 'Mummy, please put my shoes on')?

Yes, almost all the time ☐

Most of the time ☐

Some of the time ☐

Almost never ☐

Does your child get the words in the right order when she speaks?

Yes, almost all the time ☐

Most of the time ☐

Some of the time ☐

Almost never ☐

Does your child use grammatical endings (such as regular plural 's' and past tense 'ed' endings), even if occasionally incorrectly?

Yes, almost all the time ☐

Most of the time ☐

Some of the time ☐

Almost never ☐

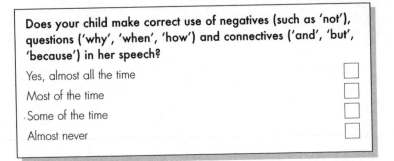

Does your child make correct use of negatives (such as 'not'), questions ('why', 'when', 'how') and connectives ('and', 'but', 'because') in her speech?

Yes, almost all the time ☐

Most of the time ☐

Some of the time ☐

Almost never ☐

If you've ticked 'almost all the time' or 'most of the time' to the above questions, your child is doing well in terms of her grammatical development.

If you've ticked mainly 'some of the time' or perhaps more worryingly 'almost never', then your child's grammar is not developing as well as it should.

4. Language in Social Situations
Does your child make use of 'social' or greeting words and phrases (such as 'hello', 'please', 'thanks') in the right situation?

Yes, almost all the time ☐

Most of the time ☐

Some of the time ☐

Almost never ☐

Does your child either repeat what she's said or put it in another way when you make it clear you haven't understood her?

Yes, almost all the time ☐

Most of the time ☐

Some of the time ☐

Almost never ☐

Does your child 'take turns' in speaking when she's talking with you or one of her friends?

Yes, almost all the time ☐

Most of the time ☐

Some of the time ☐

Almost never ☐

Does your child indicate with a look or a question when she wants you or a friend to reply or take their turn in a conversation?

Yes, almost all the time ☐

Most of the time ☐

Some of the time ☐

Almost never ☐

If you've ticked 'almost all the time' or 'most of the time', your child is beginning to understand the social rules of language that will make it easy for her to communicate with others – and that will help her make friends.

If you've ticked 'some of the time' or 'almost never', your child has not yet begun to understand the give and take of language. Although it's still early days, you will want to keep an eye on her social use of language, which is important for settling into school.

Here are some tips for helping your child's language development:

- Use **expansion and recasting**. This means that when your child says something, you expand what she has said into a longer, and probably more complex, sentence. You may also recast (rephrase and correct) what she has said if she makes a mistake, such as getting the wrong word order or making a grammatical error. For instance, your child could say, 'I gotted new blue coat,' to which you might respond with something like, 'Yes, you got a new blue coat with shiny buttons.'

- Use **reflection and reinforcement,** that is, when your child produces a well-constructed sentence, you simply repeat it back to her and then continue the conversation based on what she has already said. Your child might say, 'I had brownies at nursery,' to which you could reply, 'Great, you had brownies at nursery. Did they taste good?'
- Tell your child a little story – and then ask her to tell it back to you.
- Read stories to your child. This is one of the easiest and most enjoyable ways of helping your child's language. There is good evidence that reading stories to children helps expand vocabulary, creates awareness of grammar, and improves listening and comprehension skills. Try to read to your child every day if you can – a bedtime story is one of the best times to cuddle up together, share a story she enjoys and introduce her to the wonderful world of language and books.
- Get your child to listen to and act on instructions, for example, 'Touch the plate and then the cup.' Or 'Take a step, jump and turn around.'

● Encourage her to say 'please' and 'thank you', 'hello' and 'goodbye', and give her lots of opportunities for social chat.

Problems with Speech and Language

If you are concerned about any aspect of your child's speech or language (for instance, her nursery teacher or other family members say they can't easily understand what she says), see your GP. If the problem doesn't improve with time, then your child should be assessed by a speech and language therapist.

It is important to identify speech and language difficulties as early as possible. However, you should feel reassured to know that around half of children who have delayed speech at age three are speaking normally by five and a half.

★ **TOP TIP:** Talk, talk, talk to your child. The more she hears the spoken word and talks with other people, the better prepared her language will be for school.

3
Prepare for the Ups and Downs of School Life

For your child to be emotionally prepared for school life, he will need to feel comfortable about the idea of going to school and being left at school – and to be able to make the most of his time there. Being prepared might also mean that, when things go wrong – where there's been an upset of some kind (a lost sock, a mean remark from another child, a cross word from a teacher) – your child gets over it reasonably quickly and smoothly.

Get Your Child Emotionally Prepared
for That Important First Day

Children who know beforehand what to expect from school will be able to cope better from the start.

Here are some tips for preventing first-day worries:

- Do tell your child about the school. Describe where it is and what it looks like. Tell him about the fun aspects (pointing out what you know he is going to like, but don't give an unrealistic, fairyland picture).

- Do tell your child how he is going to get to school (walking? bus?) and who will go with him (and who will pick him up).

- Do take your child to see the school beforehand. A visit to look around and meet the teachers and other children would be best, but even the outside of the building is a help (if, for example, you know only shortly before term-time which school your child will be attending).

- Do tell your child about the school day, about lunch and timetables.

- Do encourage your child to ask questions about school – and answer as honestly as you can.
- Do ask your child what he is looking forward to most – to get him thinking positively about school.
- Do ask your child if there is anything that might bother him about his new school; you will be better able to soothe his fears if you know what he is worried about. But take care on this one – if he goes to school 'prepared' for there to be worrying things, he will be more likely to think that school is indeed a place to be feared or disliked and he may over-react even when a small problem arises. On the other hand, if he is prepared for new things and an exciting environment (and has learned the skills to cope), he should enjoy school better.

Be Ready for Separation

Preparing for separation should start early, making sure from the start that your child feels secure and happy with you. When you feel he is ready, start gradually to move your attention – and then yourself physically – away from him. Try this out at a friend's house. Can you stand and talk to your friend near your child without him worrying or demanding your attention? Then try to move further away until he cannot see you (bearing in mind that pre-school children shouldn't be left alone unattended). Next, try this at a playgroup. Start by talking to another adult, so removing the focus of your attention from your child, then gradually move yourself physically further away.

Here are some tips for leaving your child to play with a friend or at a playgroup:

- Make sure he knows who is in charge and who will look after him.
- Tell him when you are coming back (but remember pre-school age children don't have a very well-developed sense of time).
- Stick to what you have said and don't try to trick him by staying away for longer.
- Start with short separations – it's better to build up slowly and let your child tell you when you can stay away for longer.

● Comment on how well he is getting on. You are aiming to encourage his coping and to get away from the idea that he needs you there to be safe and all right.

If, after all your efforts, your pre-school child hates to be left even for short periods, this could be evidence of 'separation anxiety'. Important questions to ask are:

● Is your child feeling ill, or has there been a recent change in the family (a birth, a death, a house move) that might have unsettled him?

● Have there been arguments or problems within the family, or have you been stressed in any way? These can all worry a child and set the scene for feeling anxious or fearful generally.

● Could you have given him the 'message' that he cannot cope on his own?

● Does your child show any other specific fears (or phobias) that are preventing him from being left alone?

If any of these are true, you will need to deal with them, but do keep trying to encourage his independence.

Help Your Child to be Emotionally Intelligent

In preparing your child emotionally for school, you are also developing what is called his emotional intelligence. This is his ability to recognise others' emotions, to understand the reasons behind these emotions, and to be able to react sensitively to others' feelings.

Children need to be able to identify their own feelings before they can recognise the feelings of others.

1. Look at how well your child can recognise his own feelings:

- Can your child tell you what he is feeling when you ask him in situations that might make him angry, sad, disappointed, surprised, happy, frightened, amused? Ask: 'How does/did that make you feel?'
- For any emotions that he can't easily label, prompt by saying: 'Did that make you feel…?' (for example, sad). Is your child able to agree or disagree, and if he disagrees, can he tell you how he really is feeling? (Remember, just because you think he will or should feel a particular way in a given situation, it may not be how he actually feels.)

● Can he understand that he might feel several different emotions at the same time? For example, can he understand that it is possible to feel both hurt (emotionally) and angry; jealous but wanting to be kind; happy but also sad? Say: 'I can see/understand that you felt ... (when that happened/when she did that to you) but did you also feel a bit ...?' This may be a little advanced for some children, and you should not worry if your child is not able to do this just yet.

2. Look at how well your child can recognise the feelings of others:

● The most obvious way we judge people's feelings is by looking at their facial expressions. Check to see what emotions your child can recognise from faces and teach him how to identify what others are feeling, using the drawings overleaf.

Sad

Angry/cross

Surprised

Happy

Afraid/scared

Excited

Hurt/tearful

Shy/timid

● When your child can identify and label the emotions behind the facial expressions, go on to ask some questions about what might make the child in the picture feel unhappy, sad, angry and so on. This will help you see what depth of understanding your child has.

3. Help your child understand and react to others' feelings:

If a child knows what another child is feeling, he will be able to behave in a way that is right for that situation. On the other hand, if your child misinterprets what others are really meaning, conflicts are more likely. For example, if he thinks another child who is shouting at him is angry with *him*, he might react by crying, shouting back or even hitting out. If he thinks the other child is really upset with someone else, he might ask what the matter is, or offer to play.

Use the following scenes – and other examples of your own – to teach your child emotional understanding and how to respond to other children. These scenes will work best if you use small dolls or puppets to do the talking.

Scene 1: Here is Jack. Jack gives Ellie a present of a ... (name a toy your child would like). How does Ellie feel?

Replies showing emotional understanding of the other child are: 'Ellie feels happy/excited/cuddly.' If, however, your child says 'angry' or 'sad' or 'annoyed', ask him what makes him think Ellie would feel like that when she likes the present. From your child's answer you will understand what he is feeling in general, or he may just be remembering a present he didn't like.

If you want to check on how well your child knows what to do next, ask him a second question: 'What does Ellie say?'

Then ask: 'Jack gives Ellie a ... (name a toy less exciting to Ellie). Ellie doesn't like this present. How does Ellie feel? What should Ellie say to Jack?'

This scene will tell you whether your child understands that a) receiving presents gives pleasure; and b) when you are given something you don't like, you have to hide your feelings so as not to hurt the feelings of the person who gave it.

Scene 2: Your child cuts his finger on a knife. His friend Ben is also sitting at the table. Ben asks your child kindly if his finger hurts.

Now ask your child how he feels. Happier? Less frightened? And how was Ben feeling? Was he kind and caring?

Then suggest that Ben's reaction is quite the opposite: Ben says crossly that your child was silly to play with the knife and it serves him right. Ask how your child feels now. Sad? Angry? Unhappy that Ben isn't being nice? And Ben himself? Is he being caring now? Then ask your child if he can think of any other reason why Ben isn't being nice. (For example, is he perhaps just in a bad mood or maybe upset at all the attention being paid to your child?)

Scene 3: Here is Lee. He is building a tower. Kelly comes over and knocks it down. What does Lee think? How does he feel?

Ask your child if he thinks that Kelly knocked the tower over by accident or on purpose. Would it make any difference to what Lee did next?

Dealing with Your Child's Negative Feelings

You want your child to be able to express feelings rather than bottle them up. Those who have no outlet for their angry feelings can be like a volcano – quiet for a time then boil over with some kind of outburst. Or if the feelings are to do with being hurt or sad, your child can become miserable or start to have tummy aches or headaches caused by his feelings. If you are really worried, go to your GP. At the same time, be aware that too much encouraging of children to 'express their feelings' may make them worry more. And a cross child needs to learn that it is not okay to let his anger out by hitting or being unkind to others.

Fears and Worries

Children who are generally fearful can develop 'phobias' about things such as water (in swimming pools or baths), loud noises, animals or even being at playgroup – although this could be more about 'separation anxiety'. To get your child to understand his fears, you may need to encourage him to talk about his feelings. Be careful, of course, not to put words into his mouth. When a child says little at first, you can ask gently if this or that is what he might be feeling, and then see what he has to say. However, too much talking about fears can make them even worse. What is best is a little talking and then some action.

To help your child get over a fear, you need to get him gradually used to the situation or object. Here is an example of action you could take to get rid of a phobia of swimming pools:

1   Make lots of opportunities to do water play with your child at home.
2   Show enjoyment of water and swimming yourself (and use a favourite doll or toy animal).
3   At the same time, make trips to go past your local pool. Gradually get your child to go to the door, then inside (this may take several trips). If possible, go inside the pool building for a treat from the vending machine or snack bar – and watch the other children enjoying themselves. Bring teddy – or a friend – along too.
4   Take a trip to the shops together to choose some 'cool' swim gear.
5   When your child is ready, take him with you to the pool wearing his new swim gear to watch you swim.

6 Encourage him to dip one toe in the water – then another, then a foot – then to sit on the edge.

7 Encourage him at each stage, using praise and treats as necessary, until eventually he can get completely into the pool.

Some general tips:

- Don't show any impatience you might feel.
- Reassure him that he will be fine (but without getting into long reassuring discussions that might end up 'reinforcing' or strengthening his fears).
- Praise and even reward him with treats for each step forward.
- Make each step towards the final goal only very slightly harder than the last.
- Don't be tempted to go too fast as you don't want him getting frightened all over again.

Coping with Sibling Rivalry

Jealousy between brothers and sisters is a common childhood emotion. Many parents despair as they try to share out their attention between their children; sometimes it just seems that you can't please one child without making another feel jealous. Sometimes these jealousies can create tensions that last throughout adult life too.

Prevention is a good way to start. This should begin even before your second child is born. Help your older child to feel a useful part of the newcomer's arrival. Get him to help you prepare. Of course, he will continue to need lots of special time and attention from you; he can't be only 'Mummy's special helper'. Tell him that the baby will admire and look up to him – and how wonderful it will be for you to have your big boy with you to help. When the baby arrives, give your toddler a special present 'from' his new brother or sister.

At a later stage you can reward both children 'for getting on well together' or 'for helping each other'. This will make them more likely to be kind – more often – to each other than to squabble. Of course, some disagreements are entirely normal between brothers and sisters – and even desirable. The disagreements and squabbles between siblings can provide them with good 'practice' opportunities, in a safe environment, for dealing with conflict in the wider world.

A Word About Parental Conflict

Strife between parents is very likely to have a bad effect on children. Acknowledging your child's feelings is important, and it is a good idea to remember that he will be better off thinking well of, or at least understanding, the problems of both parents.

Do consider counselling and family conciliation if a separation (or divorce) seems to be where you are heading. If you the parents can keep a friendly relationship with each other, your child will be happier and cope better.

★ **TOP TIP:** Teach your child to develop his understanding of emotions – his own as well as others'. Use play scenes to practise the skills he needs to help him feel secure and confident.

4
Become Independent

To become independent and ready for school your child will need to be able to care for her own basic day-to-day needs. These practical self-care skills involve:

- Knowing her name and where she lives.
- Knowing how to dress and undress herself.
- Dealing with meal times, including feeding herself.
- Knowing how to manage in the toilet.
- Learning routines, such as bedtime and getting up in the morning for school.

If these skills are not in place, your child will find it much harder to achieve many of the other, more obviously school-related skills. Teachers will expect her to be 'clean and dry', able to cope at school meal times and to dress and undress for sports. Also, a child unprepared in self-care may be seen as 'babyish' by other children. This could affect friendships.

The questionnaire below covers all the different areas of self-care. See how far your child has developed in each area. For each item put a tick in the column that most closely applies to your child.

Self-Care Questionnaire			
Is your child able to:	Completely/ always	Partly/ sometimes	Not at all
Give her name?	☐	☐	☐
Give her address?	☐	☐	☐
Give her phone number?	☐	☐	☐
Give her age?	☐	☐	☐
Undress without help?	☐	☐	☐
Put on her clothes (socks/trousers/dress)?	☐	☐	☐
Do up buttons and toggles?	☐	☐	☐

	Completely/ always	Partly/ sometimes	Not at all
Fasten her shoes?	☐	☐	☐
Sit at a table to eat a meal?	☐	☐	☐
Use a spoon and fork?	☐	☐	☐
Willingly try new foods?	☐	☐	☐
Recognise (and act upon) the need to go to the toilet?	☐	☐	☐
Manage clothes in the toilet?	☐	☐	☐
Use toilet paper properly?	☐	☐	☐
Flush the toilet?	☐	☐	☐
Wash her hands after using the toilet?	☐	☐	☐
Go to bed without fuss?	☐	☐	☐
Sleep through the night without disturbing you?	☐	☐	☐

If you have ticked 'completely/always' for most items, your child is going to be well prepared for looking after herself at school.

If you have ticked mostly the 'partly/sometimes' column, it would be a good idea to work on these skills to make your child more competent.

If you have ticked the 'not at all' column for any of the items, it will be worth spending quite a lot of time getting these important skills up and running.

1. Knowing Her Own Name – and Whom to Tell

From an early age – as soon as your child is talking – you will have taught her her full name. (Be careful with nicknames as some children believe they are part of their name.) Do keep emphasising to your child that it is good to tell her name only to family members, friends, teachers and police in uniform.

2. Dressing

Your main focus is to check that your child can cope with the dressing and undressing skills needed for school. So concentrate on coats and shoes first. It is important to remember not to do everything for your child as she needs to practise in order to learn. Some children do have genuine difficulty dressing as their fine motor control is poor. (That is, their fingers don't seem to work together well to complete simple practical actions.) Don't get cross if she is slow.

Break the actions into even smaller steps if you need to. Get your child to talk her way through the steps, doing this with her at first.

Here are some tips for teaching your child dressing skills:

- Teach dressing as part of a normal routine – but make it as much fun as possible.
- Start with undressing – pulling off socks, shoes or trousers (if she is not already doing this).
- Go on to dressing, beginning with putting on tops, bottoms, dresses and socks, using backward chaining if you need to.

Backward Chaining

You help your child with the first part of an action, then she finishes it off. For example, you start by physically helping your child pull her sock up over her heel then let her pull the sock right up herself. You gradually reduce the help you give by moving your action 'backward'. For example, you next help her to put the sock over her toes – and she does all the rest.

- Teach dealing with buttons and toggles separately. If your child finds real clothes difficult, start with a special button and buttonhole on a separate piece of material (perhaps cut out from some of your old clothes). Think about the size and stiffness of the buttons and holes, and the number of buttons you use.
- Reward for achievement (every time while she is learning). Give praise, of course, but also have some small reward or 'positive reinforcer' at hand if you need to do a lot of training for a child who has difficulties.

Reward or Positive Reinforcement

This is the giving of something pleasurable to encourage particular behaviours. It is an extremely important way of helping a child learn. Almost anything your child values or likes can be used as a reward: food treats, time to watch television, a special game with you, stickers, a small toy, etc. (See Chapter 6 for full details.)

---

3. Eating

Children need to learn to use both a spoon and a fork properly. By the time your child is four, she should be using spoons and forks daily and drinking from a proper glass or cup on her own (not just from a trainer beaker).

Sharing food with others gives children the opportunity to develop many skills, including:

- Learning to sit still and attend to what she is doing.
- Listening to and responding to others round the table – and making conversation.
- Being sociable – including waiting her turn, offering food to others, and waiting for others to finish before leaving the table.

Here are some tips for developing good meal-time behaviours:

- Make the opportunity several times a week for your child to sit on a chair at a table together with one or more adults, so that she can learn all the skills above.
- Keep child portions small – young children don't need adult-sized portions.

- Don't allow frequent snacking (especially of highly fatty, salty or sugary foods) and especially don't allow 'grazing' (wandering around while eating between meals).
- Encourage your child to build up an appetite for each meal by making sure she doesn't eat anything for a couple of hours beforehand.
- Try to keep your child at the table until she has finished her meal – though don't expect her to stay at the table if your meal goes on for a long time.

What to Eat

- A healthy breakfast makes a good start to the morning. This means a choice from fresh fruit juice or fruit, low-sugar cereals (including muesli or porridge), wholemeal toast.
- Packed lunches need to be healthy – salads, sandwiches with wholemeal bread, fresh or dried fruit, unsweetened juices – to give a good boost in the middle of the day.
- Eating a wide range of foods gives the best chance of a balanced diet.

- Teach her the social skills of passing food and offering food to others around the table.
- 'Model' or demonstrate your enthusiasm for food for your child to copy.

As a parent, you will undoubtedly be very concerned if your child never seems to eat very much or will eat only a few foods. Only if her diet is very restricted will her growth be affected. However, it would be a good idea to see your GP if you are worried. Also see your GP if you cannot stop your child from eating too much of the 'wrong' kinds of food and becoming overweight.

Here are some tips to encourage eating:

- Don't expect your child to eat everything – even young children have food preferences.
- Don't tell your child she needs to eat a particular food 'because it's healthy' – label the food as 'yummy' or 'fun'.
- Give your child the same food as you eat yourself – otherwise she won't realise that 'real food' is what everyone eats. There are of course exceptions (for instance, some

very hot and spicy foods or the occasional 'special grown-up' food).

● Reward your child for eating something you want her to eat, say vegetables, with something she likes, say ice-cream.

4. Toileting

For your child to be ready to manage herself in the toilet at school, she needs to be able to:

● Recognise the physical 'urge to go' in time to get to the toilet.
● Act on this and take herself to the toilet.
● Be able to undress and dress herself again.
● Use toilet paper.
● Know how, and be able, to flush the toilet.
● Know how to wash her hands after she has been to the toilet.

Most toileting problems can be got around by having good routines. To develop skills at home, you can first make regular times to visit the toilet – before and after meals is usually best.

Add to this a regular routine of using toilet paper, then dressing, then flushing, then washing hands with soap and water.

In the beginning you may need to prompt each stage by saying, for instance, 'Now what are you going to do?' If your child replies (or acts) correctly, say, 'Great.' Only if your child is unsure or wrong, prompt her further by saying, for instance, 'Now you are going to … wash your hands' and nod for her to do it. If you can remind her simply by saying, 'You are going to w-', then just do that. When she gets to the end of the toilet routine, give the fullest praise.

Most pre-schoolers, and even some older children, have daytime accidents at least occasionally. Some may have been completely, or almost completely, dry for two or three years then suddenly start to wet their pants, say, every other day.

Wetting may start because children are worried about something, because there has been a change in routine, because there has been a mild infection, or sometimes for no apparent reason. A child could then go on wetting because the new pattern becomes a fixed habit. Once you are sure there is no physical cause (do check with your GP that there is no infection), talk to your child about what she might be worried about (friends, starting school, strange toilets). If there are no obvious worries – and even if there are – then think about a Toilet Action Plan.

Toilet Action Plan 1: Wetting

- Try not to talk to your child about being wet – but praise her for being dry and for using the toilet.
- Don't get cross when your child wets herself and give only minimum reassurance. A kindly 'Okay, let's get changed' is enough; otherwise you risk giving the wetting too much attention.
- Help her to change clothes, as necessary, with as little physical touching as possible. Be careful not to be unkind, but again don't be 'rewarding' either.
- Use a reward chart (see page 97) for being dry. If your child has been wetting several times in the day, you may need to break the day into parts (such as morning and afternoon), with a small reward for each part. If your child is also wetting at night, you could put both together on the same chart.

Sometimes children have a problem with soiling their pants. Children learn first to control their bladder during the day, but soon after also learn to control their bowels. This normally occurs between the ages of two and three. A few children just don't seem to get the idea at all. Some other children get off to a good start but then go backwards. Children may start to soil for various reasons. For example, they may become frightened of being in pain (perhaps because they have a small cut); they may have become constipated (so the soiling is mainly overflow); or they may have stopped recognising the signals from their bowels that they need to get to the toilet, and as a result get there too late.

If your child is in pain, you may need to check with a doctor. Special children's laxatives can make life easier. You may also want to look at her diet carefully to make sure she is getting enough fibre, and that she is drinking plenty of water. Then you could try the Soiling Toilet Action Plan.

Toilet Action Plan 2: Soiling

- To start with, reward your child for just sitting on the toilet – say three times a day, after meals. And, of course, give a huge amount of praise and a reward (such as a sticker) for a successful deposit!

- Once your child is able to sit on and use the toilet successfully, you can also reward her for having clean pants each evening.

- This same plan of action is fine also for children who deposit in places other than the loo. However, you may need to think about why she is doing this. Is it in defiance? Is it because she is upset about something else? You will need to be kind; if you get angry with your child (and soiling, especially in inappropriate places, arouses strong feelings) it will be harder to change the pattern. If your child is worried or upset, she will need to be helped through this too. You might find it hard simply to ignore the wrongly deposited poo. In a calm and uncritical manner, point out to your child that 'This is not the place for poo – let's put it into the loo.' Try to say no more than this as the attention in itself could become rewarding. Don't force her to clean it up, but have her accompany you to the toilet to see where it should go. Finish by reminding her that if she does her poo in the loo, she will get a sticker for her chart (keep rewarding her for sitting on the loo).

Sometimes children find it very hard to go to a toilet away from home. The basic solution is to introduce your child very gradually to other toilets. Take her to a friend's house, then reward her for just standing close to the toilet, for standing closer still, for touching the toilet lid, then for sitting on it with the lid down, then with the lid up ... then with pants down until she eventually does a pee in the (non-home) toilet.

Some children have a very strong attachment to their nappy and refuse to give it up. One way of sorting this out, with your child's agreement, is gradually to cut tiny bits off each nappy, making the one she uses smaller and smaller, until it disappears entirely. By the time you have chipped one down to almost nothing, or so it won't hold together any more, you should have solved the problem. Rewards are again the key – both for using the toilet appropriately and for having less (or no) nappy.

5. Sleeping and Bedtime Routines

Routines in general make life so much easier for children – they know what has to be done and when to do it, and will do it *automatically* once the routine is established. Sleeping and bedtime routines are a good place to start as they make such a difference to getting the school day organised.

Think about your child's day and fill in the times for each activity. It is easiest to fix on a finishing time and then work backwards in order to work out the best times for the routines to start.

Activity	Time
Getting ready for school/nursery: Time school/nursery starts Time you have to leave to get to school/nursery on time Time needed to dress and have breakfast (leave at least one hour) **Ideal wake up time is:**	

Activity	Time
Getting ready for bed:	
Ideal wake up time	
Time your child needs to spend sleeping	
Ideal lights-out time	
Time your child needs for bedtime routine (undressing, bath, reading)	
Ideal bedtime is:	

Once you have worked out your ideal times to go to bed, to have lights out, to get up and to leave the house, you have your routine set up. Next you need to get yourself, your child and your whole family geared up to work with the plan.

You can make an Evening Reward Chart (see overleaf) for your child's bedtime routine if you like. If all (or most) activities for one evening are ticked, you could reward your child with (say) five minutes of extra story time.

My Evening Chart					
Activity	Done on Time				
	Mon	Tues	Weds	Thurs	Fri
Reading time	☐	☐	☐	☐	☐
Supper time	☐	☐	☐	☐	☐
Up to bedtime	☐	☐	☐	☐	☐
Story time	☐	☐	☐	☐	☐
Lights out (sleepy time)	☐	☐	☐	☐	☐

★ **TOP TIP:** Set up – and stick to – routines. This will make life so much easier for your child and therefore for you. Following a routine doesn't mean you are rigid, boring or obsessive. Instead, all the family will be free to enjoy more independence and have more time for fun too.

5
Make Friends and Build Social Skills

During the pre-school years, your child will move away from the small world of family to the wider world of playgroup and school. How well children enjoy school depends greatly on the relationships they form with teachers and – very importantly – other children.

The following three short questionnaires will help you look at the experience your child has already had with others and how well he is managing to relate to them. Questionnaire 1 is about how often your child has the opportunity for being with others. How well your child manages his relationships with others is looked at in Questionnaires 2 and 3.

Questionnaire 1 – Opportunities for Being with People

Tick the box for each question to show the degree to which each is true for your child.

How often does your child interact with other adult family members (grandparents/uncles/aunts)?

daily ☐   once or twice a week ☐   occasionally ☐   rarely ☐

How often does your child interact with non-family adults (friends and visitors, health professionals and so on)?

daily ☐   once or twice a week ☐   occasionally ☐   rarely ☐

How often does your child see and play with family or neighbours' children (not counting brothers and sisters)?

daily ☐   once or twice a week ☐   occasionally ☐   rarely ☐

How often does your child go to playgroup, kindergarten or other organised pre-school activity group?

daily ☐   three or four times a week ☐

once or twice a week ☐   not yet started ☐

Do you feel, from your answers to these questions, that your child has had good opportunities to socialise with others, or actually very little?

good ☐   adequate ☐   little ☐

Questionnaire 2 – How Comfortable is Your Child with the People He Sees?

Is it the case that:

Your child interacts happily with *known* neighbours or professionals?

certainly ☐   sometimes ☐   not really/never ☐

Your child interacts happily with *new* adults who come to your house?

certainly ☐   sometimes ☐   not really/never ☐

Your child plays happily with children he knows (with or without an adult needing to be present)?

certainly ☐   somewhat ☐   not really/never ☐

Is it the case that:

Your child has other children he considers friends/a friend?

certainly ☐   somewhat ☐   not really/never ☐

Your child goes happily to play at other children's homes?

certainly ☐   sometimes ☐   not really/never ☐

Your child readily plays or talks with children he has *just met*?

certainly ☐   somewhat ☐   not really/never ☐

If you have ticked quite a few 'certainly' boxes in Questionnaire 2, *and* your child has had some reasonable experiences of being with other children and with new adults (Questionnaire 1), then he is managing well. If you have ticked mostly 'not really/never' boxes in Questionnaire 2, then your child may find it rather difficult to join pre-school classes and to feel comfortable with both peers and adults. If you have also ticked mostly 'rarely/not yet started/little' boxes in Questionnaire 1, then the problem may largely be due to lack of opportunity.

Questionnaire 3 – How Well Does Your Child Manage Socially at Playgroup?

For those children who have had the experience of pre-school or playgroups, look at how well things are going so far.

Does your child relate well to staff at his pre-school or nursery?

usually ☐   sometimes ☐   rarely ☐

Does your child initiate play with other children?

usually ☐   sometimes ☐   rarely ☐

Does your child respond positively when other children approach him?

usually ☐   sometimes ☐   rarely ☐

Can your child share his toys?

usually ☐   sometimes ☐   rarely ☐

Can your child wait his turn happily?

usually ☐   sometimes ☐   rarely ☐

Does your child get into fights or disagreements with other children?

most days ☐   once or twice a week ☐

once or twice a month ☐   very rarely ☐

If you have mostly ticked the 'usually' boxes (and there are only occasional fights/disagreements), then your child seems to be making a good start with his social relationships and will be well prepared when he starts school. If there are quite a few ticks in the 'rarely' boxes – or if your child gets into lots of fights and disagreements – then he needs more active help with relating to others.

The Skills Children Need to Get On with Others

The relationships children form with the adults in their lives will be different from those they form with peers. Getting on with both adults and peers is vital, and difficulties in one area can lead to difficulties in the other.

The social skills children need to get on with adults overlap with, but are not entirely the same as, those needed to get on with peers. At school, teachers expect:

- Behaviour from the child that fits in with the school routine.
- An appropriate degree of respect and politeness fitting for a non-equal relationship.
- Responsiveness to their requests and suggestions.

Talk through, demonstrate and practise these skills with your child to help him behave well with teachers. The suggestions for behaviour in Chapter 6 will help too.

To understand the important issues for social skills and friendship-making with peers, some definitions are needed. Peer acceptance, friendships, popularity and social skills (or social competence) are all terms describing how well children get on with their peers.

(Peer) acceptance refers to how well a child is accepted or maybe even tolerated by his peer group (that is, the other children in his class, but it can refer more widely to all children of his age). It doesn't mean that a child is especially liked, in the sense of being popular (see overleaf). Nor does it include his view of other children.

Children don't have to be liked by, or to like, *everyone* in a class or group to get on well. A child can keep away from those who do not like him (and whom he may well not like in return) and be happy in himself because he gets on well with everyone else. However, there could be a problem if those children who dislike a particular child start to show their feelings. This could amount to bullying, and prompt action would need to be taken (see page 74).

A *friendship* is a two-way relationship; a child likes someone who likes him back in return. Both being accepted and having friendships are important for a child's well-being.

Popularity refers to how well liked a child is. Those who are most liked or very much liked are described as popular. Being popular is not at all necessary for getting along perfectly well; general acceptance – and preferably having friends too – is more important.

Can I Help My Child Make Friends?

Parents are in a great position to encourage the skills of friendship-making and of becoming accepted – and for most children it is best not to leave these friendships to chance.

Here are some tips to help your child before he starts school:

- Make opportunities for your child to meet other children.
- Set up play dates – especially with children from your child's future class.

MAKE FRIENDS AND BUILD SOCIAL SKILLS

- Be on hand to *make sure* the play date goes well and the visiting child goes home having had a fun time.
- Cultivate old friends and make new ones yourself; the more you socialise the more your child is likely to copy you and learn how to make and keep friends.
- Actively practise the social skills of friendship-making (see below for some ideas on how to do this).
- Continue all these throughout the early school years too.

Develop the Skills of Mixing and Friendship-Making

Here are some common social situations. Use dolls or puppets to help your child practise the skills needed for mixing with other children (in groups). For each scene examples of *competent coping strategies* and *poor coping strategies* are given. Praise your child for all appropriate strategies he suggests or acts out. If he suggests only poor strategies, tell him about competent strategies that work better – and use the dolls or puppets to demonstrate.

Scene 1: Your child wants a toy another child is playing with.

Show two dolls (of the same sex as your child – call them, say, 'Max' and 'John'). Say, 'Here's Max. Max is playing with this fire engine. Now John wants a turn to play with the fire engine. Max has been playing with it for a long time. What can John do to get a turn to play with the fire engine? What can John say?'

Good suggestions from your child might include:

- I'd ask him nicely if I can have a turn now.
- I'd say, 'I'll give you this toy and you give me yours.'
- I'd say, 'Can I have a go in a bit?' (Specific amounts of time, such as five minutes, are hard concepts for many pre-schoolers to manage, as is patience if he has to wait longer than he expects.

Poor strategies might include:

- I'd snatch it away from him.
- I'd hit him.
- I'd cry.

- I'd tell him he is mean and horrid.
- I'd tell the teacher to make him give it to me.

You can then go on to suggest to your child that some strategies will work better than others. Act out the good strategies to help him cope more effectively.

Scene 2: Joining in play. Tilly and Kate are playing with some bricks. Chelsy wants to play with Tilly and Kate too. What can Chelsy do or say so that she can play with them?
Good suggestions are:

- 'Do you want some yellow bricks from the basket? I'll get them for you.'
- 'Can I drive my car on your road?'
- 'You've made a great farm – can I make a field for the cows?'

Poor suggestions are:

- 'Those aren't your bricks.'
- 'I want to play with them now.'
- 'You are mean cos you aren't letting me play.'

This joining-in scene is quite a tricky one, and the skills required are complex and sophisticated. Young children need to learn that first 'initiations' or attempts to join others will sometimes get a negative response. This doesn't mean that your child isn't liked. He will need to learn that what he has to do is not give up but try later on or use another approach.

Here are some tips for making initiations:

- Teach your child to ask: 'Please can I play?' and not just barge in.
- Suggest to your child that he watches a little, then says something nice, like: 'That's a really cool tower' or 'You make the train go so fast.'
- Suggest to your child he can do something else to move things forward, like making an exciting suggestion such as: 'I'm a wizard and we can fly to the castle.'

The key is for your child not to feel defeated or miserable at being left out if (when!) his first attempts to join in fail. Of course, other children can feel that too many initiations from one child are just annoying – at that moment. Your child needs to develop the self-confidence to say and feel, 'Okay, another time' – and come back later.

Scene 3: Making a new friend. This is Ed and this is Jason. How can Ed make friends with Jason?

Good strategies are:

- Go up to him and say, 'Hello, what's your name? My name is ...'
- Say, 'Do you want to play with the bricks with me?'
- Tell him he has built a really good model.
- Ask him to join in the game with me and my friends.
- Answer his questions.

Poor strategies are:

- Do nothing.
- Say, 'You look silly standing there.'
- Say, 'You are new. I don't like you.'

When you have done this scene, ask your child, 'Now, how can *you* make friends with Jason?'

Leaving Your Child at a Playgroup or School

Here are some tips:

- Prepare your child in advance: the prepared child is more likely to think that he is able to join in and that he has the skills to cope.
- Don't show your worry – it can transmit itself to your child and make him behave in more anxious ways too.
- Encourage your child to join in social activities but take care not to force him. Don't say, 'Come on, Sam, don't just stand there. Join in!'
- Avoid suggesting he can't cope. Don't say, 'Don't worry. You don't have to play with anyone if you don't want to,' or, 'I'll stay and play with you if you don't want to play with those girls right now.'

Children Who Find It Difficult to Relate to Others

Children don't have to play or be with others all the time to be getting on perfectly well. However, if your child is anxious, fearful or socially unskilled, then this is a different story because he might be, or become, unhappy. Children who are not making any initiations would certainly need some help. You could keep practising more scenes using dolls or role-playing with your child.

But some youngsters with difficulties in relating to others may also use language oddly or show 'obsessive' and repetitive behaviour. Such children could have a developmental disorder. Check this out using the following questionnaire.

Have you noticed any of the following in your child?

	Yes	No
He shows little interest in people or does not try to engage with them like others do.	☐	☐
Sometimes he seems 'deaf' and doesn't react to things you say.	☐	☐
He rarely looks at you when you speak to him (poor eye contact).	☐	☐
When you ask him something like 'Do you want a biscuit?' he replies, 'You want a biscuit,' not using the correct pronoun 'I'.	☐	☐

	Yes	No
He is distressed by other children, or allows himself to be played with passively like a doll, or is ignored by them.	☐	☐
He insists on 'sameness' and dislikes changes to routines.	☐	☐
He has fixations or obsessions with unusual things like vacuum cleaners.	☐	☐
He likes to do or say the same things over and over again and becomes distressed if stopped.	☐	☐
He seems to have no ability to 'mind read'; that is, being able to view something from another person's point of view.	☐	☐
He says 'odd' things that are irrelevant to what is going on.	☐	☐
He finds it hard to keep a conversation going, including turn-taking and sticking to the subject without going off in a new direction.	☐	☐

If you have marked 'Yes' to a number of these items, it might be that your child has a social-communication difficulty. This would need further investigation, since some of these children also have problems with the use of language and may be described as having an 'autistic spectrum disorder'. If you are concerned that your child shows difficulties in these areas, ask your GP to refer you for a specialist opinion, for example with a Child Development Team.

Aggression, Conflict and Bullying

Aggression – or aggressive behaviours – are negative behaviours that may be directed at peers, adults, property or a combination of the three. Although it is not unusual for young children to show aggression from time to time, it is unacceptable when physical or psychological harm is caused to others. From a very early age, children need to be taught that causing such harm cannot be allowed or tolerated.

Conflict is different from aggression. Conflict is disagreement with another, where one person does or says something to which the other objects. Conflicts can occur either with or without aggression, and both are part of normal development. In the toddler years, girls and boys get involved in similar amounts of conflict. From the age of three or four, boys are more likely to find themselves in conflict situations than girls.

Conflicts can have a positive side too because they give children the opportunity to learn the skills of good *conflict resolution*, essential for adult life.

Bullying involves one child frightening another by repeated verbal, psychological or physical aggression. The term 'bullying' rightly arouses strong emotions in adults; no parent wants their child to be 'got the better of' and hurt by another. Likewise, if your child gets the reputation for being a bully to others, it will be unpleasant too. Many children's lives have been made utterly miserable by being picked on, teased and consistently bullied.

Here are some tips to help prevent your child from becoming a victim of bullying:

- Role-play social situations (see page 66) and talk about ways to deal with children who bully.
- Teach the skills of sharing and co-operating, the art of joining in play and other friendship-making strategies.
- Encourage him to try to initiate, to feel fine if he can't find a way to join in a group he wants to join, and to feel self-confident enough to try more than one strategy.

- Help him to make 'allies' in his group – make friends with other parents and their children from your child's playgroup or kindergarten and invite home both parents and child.

- Try not to be too overprotective (see Chapter 3). This makes children more anxious and dependent – and appear vulnerable to potential bullies.

- Help him to learn coping skills such as avoiding 'reinforcing' the bullies. If the victim reacts by 'giving in', crying, looking miserable or generally acting like a victim, this can reinforce or act like a green light to the bully to do it again.

- Reassure your child that being bullied is not *his* fault – and he must always tell an adult.

- Remind yourself that some children have a more anxious and fearful temperament. Some look physically frail or small. These children might need much more input from you to make sure they have the skills and allies to cope.

Here are some tips to help prevent your child becoming a bully:

- Don't give him the message that it is okay to cause hurt. It is important that he can put himself in others' shoes so that he avoids saying or doing things that other children find hurtful. If you let your child think it is fine not to think of others but only of himself then that is what your child will do.

- Don't be too angry or punitive with him. If you do then you are 'modelling' bullying behaviour. This will only lead to him bullying more. (See Chapter 6 on parenting style.)

- Do notice if he calls other children names or behaves in ways likely to frighten or upset others. Do talk – gently – to him about how upset the other child might feel.

- Do suggest something kind that he could do or say to make the other child feel better, to repair the hurt caused. Get him to think of helpful things for himself.

- Do praise (and even reward) him for being kind, for saying sorry, for reacting in non-aggressive ways when the game does not go his way, and so on.

⭐ **TOP TIP:** Take an active role in helping your child develop social skills and make friends with the parents of other children in the class. Practise friendship-making and friendship-keeping using dolls or puppets and play scenes.

Learn to Behave

If children are to become easy to get on with and a pleasure to be around, in adults' eyes this depends on how 'well behaved' they are. In the early pre-school years, crying and saying 'no' and having temper tantrums are a normal part of development. But by the time children start school they will need to be able to listen to you at home and to do what they are told. And in a class full of children teachers will expect even more.

Behaving well at school means that:

● Your child should be able to stop doing something instantly (or reasonably quickly) when asked. This is essential –

otherwise she could, without realising it, be placing herself or others in a position of danger.

- Your child should be able to do what is asked of her in a range of other situations too (such as waiting quietly, fetching something, concentrating without distracting others, getting changed for sports). Her ability to do this is known as 'compliance'. Children who are frequently 'non-compliant' will be considered a problem.

- Your child should be able to control her negative feelings. Children who don't may be seen as aggressive and immature.

In a classroom, children whose behaviour is not in line with the rest may well find themselves not liked by both adults and peers. This in turn can lead to poor self-esteem and unhappiness. If your child's behaviour already seems problematic, it is important to take action now to help her to be happy and manage well when she gets to school.

Complete the following questionnaire to look at how well behaved your child is.

For each question, tick the behaviour that comes closest to describing your child.

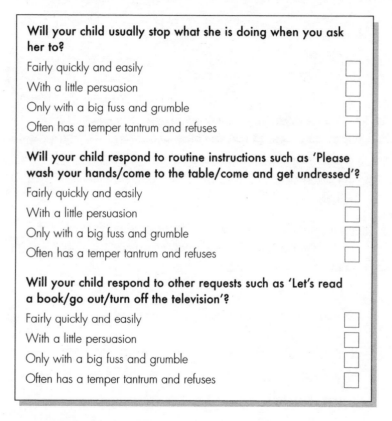

Will your child usually stop what she is doing when you ask her to?

Fairly quickly and easily ☐

With a little persuasion ☐

Only with a big fuss and grumble ☐

Often has a temper tantrum and refuses ☐

Will your child respond to routine instructions such as 'Please wash your hands/come to the table/come and get undressed'?

Fairly quickly and easily ☐

With a little persuasion ☐

Only with a big fuss and grumble ☐

Often has a temper tantrum and refuses ☐

Will your child respond to other requests such as 'Let's read a book/go out/turn off the television'?

Fairly quickly and easily ☐

With a little persuasion ☐

Only with a big fuss and grumble ☐

Often has a temper tantrum and refuses ☐

Does your child damage/hit/kick/attempt to destroy objects?

Only exceptionally or not at all ☐

Now and again ☐

Regularly ☐

Does your child deliberately hit/kick/bite or in other ways attempt physically to hurt any other person?

Only exceptionally or not at all ☐

Now and again ☐

Regularly ☐

If 'now and again' or 'regularly' to either of the previous two questions, what have the circumstances generally been?

Unprovoked ☐

Clearly provoked ☐

To whom have the aggressive acts been directed?

To you (one or both parents) ☐

To brother or sister ☐

To other children (known? just met?) ☐

To other adults (what type of relationship?) ☐

Does your child use bad language (name-calling, swearing) directed at other people?

Only exceptionally or not at all ☐

Now and again ☐

Regularly ☐

Does your child attempt to harm herself such as by biting herself or pulling out her hair?

Only exceptionally or not at all ☐

Now and again ☐

Regularly ☐

Does your child deliberately do 'naughty' things like hiding others' possessions, taking sweets when asked not to, or throwing toys around when asked to clear up?

Only exceptionally or not at all ☐

Now and again ☐

Regularly ☐

If you find that your child (either most of the time or frequently):

- won't comply with routine tasks without making a fuss;
- won't readily comply with most requests;
- is deliberately 'naughty' (as opposed to occasionally 'mischievous'); or
- is physically or verbally aggressive towards objects and/or people

then clearly her behaviour is a real problem that has to be dealt with.

If the behaviours that concern you are largely provoked – usually by a brother or sister – then you could try to find ways of removing or lessening the provocation, even if you still have to deal with the behaviours themselves.

If your child is regularly hurting herself deliberately, you might want to consider whether she is in fact showing signs of emotional distress. Think what possible causes there might be and use Chapter 3 to help you.

What do you do when your child misbehaves?

Think of what you did the last couple of times your child misbehaved. Look at the questions opposite and tick any of the boxes that apply.

Did you:

Grin and bear it and say nothing? ☐

Make excuses for her – she's so tired/frustrated/sickly/in the shadow of her brother/sister – but do nothing? ☐

Spend a long time explaining to her why what she did was wrong? ☐

Punish her by depriving her of something? ☐

Send her to her room/out of your room? ☐

Tell her off firmly and leave it at that? ☐

End up having a shouting match about what she has done? ☐

Lose your cool completely and shout furiously or lash out? ☐

Other..? ☐

How effective did you feel your strategies were – and are – in general?

Effective overall? ☐

Sometimes effective, sometimes not? ☐

Often or regularly ineffective? ☐

As you think about your general effectiveness, remind yourself too of what happened *after* each incident.

- Did your child seem to listen to you and say sorry – but then do the same thing again soon after?
- Did she listen but then do some different naughty thing soon after?
- Did she do as you asked but carried on making a lot of fuss?

Constant misbehaviour is very wearying for parents. To avoid – or at least reduce – stress and strain it is so much better to have an effective plan of action to prevent difficult and naughty behaviours from occurring in the first place and to have a clear strategy for when they do happen. The steps below are aimed at *prevention*.

Steps for Improving Your Child's Behaviour: Parenting Style

First look at your general approach to discipline and managing (or parenting) your child – your 'parenting style'.

1. Know your parenting style

Look at these four different styles of parenting and think which most closely describes yours.

- The *authoritarian style* is characterised by strong insistence that the child behaves well, or achieves the parents' expected standards. The methods used involve strong control, more of a 'do as I say ... because I told you to' approach. These parents use criticism and punishment to achieve control with relatively little praise, explanations or discussion.
- The *permissive style* is characterised by a laid-back approach, with no, or few, expectations of the child: what she does is fine, regardless of her real capability to make decisions. The parents are warm and caring but may not notice all the child's needs or attend sufficiently to them.
- The *uninvolved style* is characterised by a distancing of the parents from much of what the child is doing. The child has to 'bring herself up', 'make her own decisions' and 'do her own thing'.
- The *authoritative style* is characterised by a balanced, caring and warm approach to the child. Standards expected for behaviour (that is, 'boundaries') are in place, but the demands made are reasonable and fair. This approach involves sensitivity and attention to the child's needs plus acknowledgement of her efforts using discussions,

explanations and negotiations to achieve goals. The parent is in control but in the manner of a 'guider' rather than either a 'law enforcer' or, at the other extreme, an equal 'pal'.

Research studies have shown that an *authoritative* approach – firm but fair, with clear boundaries, warm and attentive, both accepting and involved but sensitive to the child's needs – is best.

2. Become an authoritative parent

To become an authoritative parent yourself you need to develop both **good nurturance** and **moderate control**.

Good nurturance means parents' caring behaviours that are aimed at being encouraging and supportive of their children.

Here are some tips to develop good nurturance:

- Make lots of opportunities to have friendly and fun play and experiences with your child. Encourage her (but do not force her) to choose some of these activities (rather than just your own preferences).
- Be considerate of your child's wishes and needs (don't insist that only the adults' views count).

- Show an interest in your child's daily activities. Talk about the other children at her playgroup and the toys she played with, the clothes she likes, the DVDs she has watched and so on (this is all good for language too – see Chapter 2).

- Respect your child's point of view. You do not have to agree with her views, but try to acknowledge them as 'interesting', 'intelligent' or 'imaginative'.

- Tell your child how proud you are of her for each of her achievements and milestones. Keep a file for all her certificates and programmes for the shows she's in – one with transparent envelopes works well (her 'Achievements File').

- Show your affection – regularly kiss, cuddle, hug and affectionately touch your child, boys as well as girls. It is not 'babyish' or 'unmanly' to show affection.

- When asked an unreasonable request, listen to your child and rather than just turning her down, offer explanations and alternatives – and possible compromises.

- Find lots of different ways of making your child feel valued and not stupid – tell her what a great helper she is to her younger brother/how clever she is for doing or saying something.

● And always give lots of praise to show your approval.

To become an authoritative parent you will also need to develop moderate control – that is, discipline that is neither too heavy-handed nor too free.

Here are some tips to develop moderate control:

● Offer reasons and explanations for the requests/demands/ expectations you have of your child and try not to insist 'You have to do it because I say so…' (although there are going to be times that you will just have to do this).
- She will understand and behave better with a clear but brief explanation.
- Pick a quiet moment to talk about right and wrong and why parents get cross (too much talking at the moment you are cross with your child may only reinforce the behaviours you are trying to stop).

● Notice and acknowledge good behaviour.
- Telling your child how well she has done, in a tone of voice that shows you are pleased, will help a lot to make her more likely to do again the good things that pleased you.
- Try not to say too much when a child is doing wrong (even

such remarks as 'That behaviour makes me sad' gives too much attention to the behaviour).

- When your child misbehaves, try to look at both your and her view of the problem and reach a 'just' and fair solution.
  - If the misbehaviour involves two children in conflict, it is best to listen to both sides, preferably in such a way as to let each feel heard (and to try not to label either as 'to blame'), then move on.

- Use 'consequence-based' discipline – expect your child to make up for her wrong-doing – where possible.
  - If your child has made a mess on the floor (deliberately) then it is reasonable to expect her to help with at least a bit of the cleaning up.
  - The consequence cannot always fit the damage done (and sometimes small children can inflict mighty large damage with a single careless gesture), but it does have to take into account the child's intentions, her limited ability to think ahead, and of course her age.
  - Psychological hurts (name-calling, teasing) or physical hurts to others (kicking, knocking over) should never be dealt with by kicking or name-calling back.

- Your aim – the ideal consequence – is to get her to apologise or to say she feels sad that she did it.

● Avoid harsh physical punishment (like smacking or shutting her away in a room on her own for more than a few minutes – but see Time Out below), ridiculing or otherwise putting down your child, or attacking her sense of self-worth. Also avoid making unpleasant threats – like saying you will take away all her toys or you will never play with her again – as this will only have a bad effect on your relationship and not help her behaviour.

● Try to keep your cool – if you can't, how will she? Think ahead about strategies for managing your anger (look away, count to 10, take a couple of slow breaths). Think 'cool' – remember you are an experienced adult and must be able to find other ways to get around your child's annoying or naughty behaviour (and be aware that most children can drive the calmest parents wild at some stage).

● Find ways to make sure your child believes that you really love and want her and that you believe in her; it is only the *behaviour* you don't like – not her.

- Apologise when you have been in the wrong (not least because this will teach her to apologise too).
- Again, use positive reinforcement including praise, reward and approval to change her behaviour and to help her to comply.

Steps for Improving Your Child's Behaviour: Using a Reward Action Plan

The next steps will help you to manage difficult behaviour when it happens. To set up a plan of action you first need to be clear about exactly what the problems are. The best way to do this is to make some *observations* about what is actually happening. Observing and recording your own child's behaviour can be a tricky business for a busy parent in the middle of looking after her (and maybe other children too). Either write everything down afterwards when you have a quiet moment (but this means you could forget some bits) or, if you can, do jot down some notes at the time things are happening. Alternatively, if a friend is on hand, ask her to help out.

1. Observe your child's behaviour (and how you deal with it, too)

Look at the steps below to help you make a record of what is actually going on when your child is misbehaving – your **ABC** record chart. You will need a large sheet of paper or a notebook. Copy the chart on page 94 to make it easier for you to see what is happening – note down what your child did and how each incident started and ended. (Try to avoid letting your child see what you are doing, so that things take a 'natural course'.)

- Decide on the behaviours that you want to keep track of and note these in the **Behaviour (B)** column. They would typically be temper tantrums (TT for short) or separately kicking (K), screaming (S), biting (B), hitting (H), pushing (P), throwing (TH), not doing what she is told (non-compliance or NC). These will be your 'target behaviours' that you want to change.
- When your child does any of the target behaviours, fill in the Date, Time and Place column on your chart.
- Think carefully about what happened before the (behaviour) incident started. These are the **Antecedents (A)**. For example, you asked your child to come and sit down to eat

a meal. She was playing with her train and asked for a few minutes more. Half an hour later she still refused to come to the table ... Write this down in the **A**ntecedents column.

● Write down, too, any 'context' antecedents – things that happened, say, earlier that morning or even on a previous day, that might be relevant. For example, an older brother wouldn't come to the table when asked – and he got away with it. This information can be helpful for you in thinking about how to alter the things in the environment that act as triggers for the problem behaviours.

● Now for the **Consequences (C)**, that is, all that happened after the behaviour(s). Record in the **C**onsequences column what you did or said, what your child then did or said and what you did next. Sometimes, as a result of what you did, your child may show another (or more of the same) of your target behaviours. (For example, you told her to go to her room and she kicked you or the wall.) Be honest – if you lose your cool and shout at your child, write that down too.

● Keep recording all that's happening in the **B**ehaviour and **C**onsequences columns until the whole behaviour incident ends.

Here is a blank **ABC** Chart for you to copy:

Date/Time/ Place	**A**ntecedents	**B**ehaviour	**C**onsequences

When you have made your observations for long enough (maybe a week without trying to do anything different) and have got a good idea of the pattern of what goes on, ask yourself the following questions:

- How often did you observe the target behaviours?
  - Several times a day?
  - Once a day?
  - Two or three times a week?
  - About once a week?
  - Not observed at all lately?
- Did your child get over an incident:
  - Very quickly and easily (it only lasted a short time)?
  - Fairly quickly and easily?
  - With difficulty?
  - With great difficulty (it all went on for a long time)?

The answers to these questions give you some idea of the extent of the problem – and how much of a problem it is for you. If you feel things are getting on top of you, that your child's problematic behaviour is happening too often and that it is hard to get the incident sorted, then you need to take some action.

Before you start a plan of action take stock of your family situation:

- Solutions to improving your child's behaviour are likely to work better if you feel supported by a good network of family and friends.
- If you are a single parent and feeling insufficiently supported or if you and your partner are together but are having relationship difficulties of your own, these situations are likely to make it harder for you to do the job of parenting as well as you might like.
- Competition between brothers and sisters for parents' attention is common. Try to find some time alone with each child on a regular basis if you possibly can.

2. Set up a reward action plan

Start by setting up a structured plan based on rewards for behaviour that you want to see your child doing. At the same time move away from angry words or punishments.

a) Prepare a reward chart

Charts are a handy way of keeping a record and showing your child (and you) what good progress has been made. Charts allow children more opportunities to feel good about themselves.

Charts can be used for lots of different kinds of behaviour. With young children, charts need to be simple and clear to understand. You can use stickers, ticks, colouring in or marbles in cylindrical tubes, so one tick or sticker (or whatever) forms your basic 'unit' of reward (or 'reinforcement').

Example reward chart

The chart overleaf shows how a child can earn a smiley face sticker for each of three morning behaviours. She can also earn a special sticker (call it a 'special bumper sticker' or whatever else takes your or her fancy) after being successful for *all* her (three) main targets on the same day (a 'Full House'). Do some simple drawings (such as a picture of a bed for getting up) to help your child understand her targets.

When Jade gets up in the morning

	Mon	Tues	Wed	Thurs	Fri	Sat	Sun
1. Get up when Mum asks		☺		☺	☺		
2. Eat breakfast (in 15 mins – without dawdling)		☺	☺	☺	☺		
3. Dress self ('happily')			☺	☺	☺		
'Full house' – GREAT				💥	💥		

b) Make rewards work

The effectiveness of a reward plan depends almost entirely on how it is set up and carried out. Here are some tips:

- Always give *spoken praise* (such as 'well done', 'you did a great job') in addition to something like a food treat, a sticker or a small toy.
- Give rewards *immediately* after the child has done what you want her to do.
- Be *consistent* in your approach – don't forget to give the reward each time your child does what you ask.

- Keep the *size* of the reward in line with the behaviour. Small improvements in behaviour deserve small rewards – like a sticker for trying a mouthful of new food. Breakthrough behaviours (like using the toilet on her own for the first time) would justify something larger.

- Find rewards that are exciting and interesting for your child. Rewards don't have to be expensive toys. Time spent with you planning a special game, a short outing, watching a favourite DVD, all make good rewards.

- Don't give the reward if it hasn't been earned. However, if your target looks to be too high for your child to manage, it is good to reward her for being 'almost there' at the start of a new reward plan. As your child's behaviour improves, you should reward her for complete (rather than partial) success in achieving the target.

- Have clear targets (such as reducing temper tantrums, using cutlery at meal times, complying with requests) and don't use vague terms like 'being good' or 'not naughty'. Your child needs to know exactly what she has to do to earn her reward.

c) Keep the plan on track

Expect an action plan to take up to several weeks. But if you feel it's not working well enough, here are some tips to get things moving again:

- Check that you have made the target behaviours clear enough and broken down into sufficiently small steps for your child to manage easily.

- Consider giving a greater reward for certain things. For example, it might be better to give, say, three stars or smiley faces instead of only one for a big thing like 'keeping her cool' when provoked by a brother or sister.

- Give extra bonuses for achieving the target for, say, three days in a row – call it a 'super bumper sticker'.

- Do not remove any stars/smiley faces/stickers that your child has earned because you are cross with her. She put in the effort, so deserved them.

- Make sure your charts are sufficiently interesting and colourful (and therefore rewarding) for a pre-school child.

- Have you remembered to complete the charts every day? (You and not your child should be in charge of this.)

- Have you (both parents preferably) had time to admire with your child her chart and her achievements?
- Have you checked with her that the rewards are indeed rewarding, or if she has any questions about the plan?
- Have you (or some relative) been giving extra toys/goodies recently, so removing the incentive for your child to 'earn' things for herself?
- Could it be that you are sometimes still 'rewarding', and so reinforcing, the very behaviour you are trying to stop or reduce? Giving attention to the naughty behaviour – or an unearned reward to avoid a tantrum – will only teach her that she can still be naughty but it doesn't really matter.

Steps for Improving Your Child's Behaviour: Using Time Out and Ignoring

Sometimes a reward plan is not enough. For very naughty behaviours that hurt other people or for constant refusal to listen (non-compliance) or for temper tantrums, you could also add 'Time Out'.

Time Out is not meant to be a punishment but is more a 'cooling off' period when **you do not interact at all** with your child. It can be a very effective way of helping her change her behaviour (and for you to keep your cool and your sanity). However, it is best not to start using this method unless you have a positive reward plan in place. This is because it is so much better to work on the principle of rewarding, of noticing your child's efforts, of talking to her about what she has done right and not about what she has done wrong.

Here are some tips for setting up a Time Out plan:

- Set up the positive reward plan for your child and have it going for at least a week. She needs to see that, if she sticks to what she agreed to do, she will get something fun and you will be pleased.
- Next explain to your child that if she does certain things – things that you would like to help her not to do, and that she seems not yet able to stop herself from doing (such as yelling, biting, hitting, shouting, refusing to get dressed – be specific), you will put her into Time Out.
- When your child next starts to misbehave, go into your

Time Out sequence. First ask her to stop or, better still, suggest she does something else like come and eat her breakfast or get dressed. (It is better to phrase your words in a positive way to avoid 'Don't' or 'Stop' if you can.) If she reacts positively, say 'Well done' and just carry on as normal with whatever you are doing (and remember to reward her later for having behaved as you asked her to). But if she continues to kick/shriek/refuse to do as you ask, say, 'I've asked you to keep your cool, etc., and will have to put you in Time Out if you don't come/do etc. now.' This is your *one* warning to her. If she stops then fine, but if she continues with the same behaviour, say (without any further discussion or negotiation), 'I am going to put you into Time Out.' You can occasionally add a *brief* comment or explanation such as 'It's unkind to hurt people' but keep most of the talking for the beginning, when you are explaining why you will be using Time Out.

- Now put your child into the area you have chosen for Time Out. Make sure your child is safe and the area not too unpleasant. Sometimes just putting her outside the door of the room you are in is simplest, or even on a special Time Out chair. Do not look at her or say anything else. If your child removes herself from Time Out, immediately and firmly (without any discussion) return her, holding the door shut or even holding her (with minimum force) if necessary. Once your child is in Time Out, ignore what you can (like the door kicking or opening the door) until it is time for her to come out.

- For a pre-school age child, aim to leave her in Time Out for up to five minutes. Then, as soon as she is quiet, say in a calm tone of voice, 'You can come out of Time Out now,' perhaps adding, 'Well done for calming down.'

- Repeat the process as often as you need to. Have lots of fun in between, and don't refer back to the Time Out or talk about the behaviours that led up to it.

- Be warned – when you first set up a Time Out plan at home, some children protest by shrieking and crying *more*. You cannot let your child come away from Time Out until she is quiet. You have to find only a few seconds of your child being quiet for you to say, 'You can come out of Time Out now.'

- Do not be alarmed or concerned if your child says she doesn't want to come out of Time Out. This is also a protest – ignore it and she will come out eventually (do not plead with her to come out!).

'Ignoring' is useful for relatively minor annoying behaviours designed to wind you up – like using bad language or whining. Ignoring, which means ignoring a child's behaviour rather than ignoring the child, is actually more difficult than many people think. A look, a tone of voice, a comment can all show your child that ignoring her behaviour is not what you are actually doing!

Here are some tips for ignoring your child's behaviour:

- Say nothing about the behaviour at all; even comments like 'I am ignoring you while you are ...' mean you are giving attention to the behaviour.
- Don't look at your child – or, at least, don't let your eyes meet.
- Make no gestures or body movements such as throwing your hands up in despair that might let your child think

that you have, in fact, taken note of the behaviour – which is just what she wanted.

TOP TIP: Noticing and rewarding good behaviour is much more effective than getting cross, punishing or making threats you cannot keep when your child is naughty or difficult. Best of all is prevention. Develop an authoritative parenting style and you will reduce the number of unpleasant incidents you have to deal with.

7

Learn to Concentrate

Attention is so important to school life, it is well worth preparing your child for the listening and concentrating he will have to do in the classroom. Between the ages of three and six years, you can expect to see huge improvements in your child's attention, including:

- Being more able to work on structured activities and play.
- Increasing the length of his concentration span from a few minutes at age three to around half an hour at age six (at least in structured one-to-one activities with an adult).
- Being increasingly able to stay with the task and not become easily distracted.

- Being increasingly able to work on his own for short periods.
- Being able by the age of four to control his impulsivity – that is, being able to hold back from an action he wants to do but has been told not to.
- Being able to control his activity level and not to be 'hyper' or overactive.

How Well Can Your Child Concentrate?

The questionnaire below will show you how well your child can concentrate. For each item, tick the box that best describes your child's level of attention.

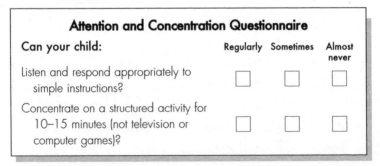

Attention and Concentration Questionnaire

Can your child:	Regularly	Sometimes	Almost never
Listen and respond appropriately to simple instructions?	☐	☐	☐
Concentrate on a structured activity for 10–15 minutes (not television or computer games)?	☐	☐	☐

	Regularly	Sometimes	Almost never
Watch cartoons for 20 minutes or more?	☐	☐	☐
Sit at the table during meal times (until he has finished eating)?	☐	☐	☐
Finish (short) tasks or games once started?	☐	☐	☐

How Active (or Overactive) is Your Child?

Again, tick the box that shows your child's level of activity.

Activity Questionnaire			
Does your child:	Regularly	Sometimes	Almost never
Run around and appear to be always on the go?	☐	☐	☐
Interrupt others or intrude inappropriately (for instance, poking or prodding)?	☐	☐	☐
Make a lot of noise or talk constantly?	☐	☐	☐
Have difficulty taking turns?	☐	☐	☐
Fidget and squirm?	☐	☐	☐
Appear to act 'without thinking'?	☐	☐	☐

If you have ticked most of the items as 'regularly' on the Attention and Concentration questionnaire or 'almost never' on the Activity questionnaire, then your child is developing good concentration and self-control.

If you have mostly ticked the 'sometimes' column, your child is doing quite well, but you could help bring him along a little further in readiness for school.

If you have lots of ticks in the 'almost never' column on the Attention and Concentration questionnaire, or the 'often' column on the Activity questionnaire (and your child is four or older), you have some way to go to prepare your child for what is needed in school.

Generally speaking, boys are a little slower to develop their concentration skills and may be more easily distracted than girls.

Attention Action Plan

This Action Plan will help you help your child to:

- listen attentively
- look attentively

- finish set activities or tasks
- work towards a longer concentration span
- think before acting

Before you start the Action Plan, you need to think about the following questions:

- Who is going to run the plan (mother, father, carer, grand-parent)?
- Where? You will need a quiet corner away from other family members or children.
- When? It is best to pick a time when your child is not hungry or tired. Shortly after returning from pre-school or even first thing in the morning may be best.
- How often? Short daily concentration training sessions are best.

Next, collect all the materials you will need:

- Kitchen timer – get a fun one, like a hen.
- Paper, pencils, crayons, scissors, glue, sticky papers, puzzles, books, etc.

- Make some red and green cards. Red for 'stop and wait' and green for 'go ahead'.

Here are some tips for lengthening your child's concentration span:

- When you start the first concentration session, make sure you choose a session length that is right for your child's concentration span. If you think his concentration span is very short, it is perfectly fine to start with only five minutes. This is especially true for children as young as three to four years. A child of five to six years could probably manage about 15 minutes (with activity changes). The starting session length is called the 'baseline'. The aim of the Action Plan is to increase the session length bit by bit. Think of your plan lasting weeks rather than days. You should aim for a concentration span of around 30 minutes by the time your child is five or six.

- Even if he is not doing the set activity, you should still praise him for just sitting at the table. If five minutes seems difficult for your child, you might need to set your activity period for only two minutes. He needs to experience success so that he will want to do it again.

- Once you have decided on the length of the session, stick to it. You should time it carefully. Do not overstep the time limit, even if your child is working well.

- Most young children are uncertain of concepts of time and don't know how long five or ten minutes is. If this is the case, it may be helpful to use a kitchen timer with a buzzer or alarm which can be set to signal the end of the session.

- Ideally the session should be ended while your child is still interested and co-operative, not when he is bored, frustrated or having a tantrum.

- Before you think of lengthening the session, your child needs to be working consistently and confidently for the baseline time period for at least a week. When you do increase the length, do so by a very small amount.

- Before you start giving instructions, make sure your child is looking at you.

- Make sure that the activities you do with your child are interesting and enjoyable.

- Make sure the activities you choose are not too hard for your child – you want him to feel pleased with himself afterwards.
- Make sure you keep on telling your child how well he is doing when he is working nicely with you.
- Do use a reward programme (see Chapter 6 for more details). As always, praise is important, but stickers can also be given for staying on task until the timer buzzer goes.

Here are some tips for coping with impulsivity:

- Before you start an activity, first make sure your child is looking at you and ready to listen to you.
- Keep your instructions and demonstrations short and clear.
- Praise your child for listening or watching carefully. Say, 'Well done – you watched really carefully.'
- Work out with him a special signal that means 'stop and wait' – for instance, using the red card. If, when you are explaining or demonstrating something, he tries to start the activity, hold up the red card. Praise your child for waiting, finish your instructions, then show him the green card as the signal for him to start the activity.

- Use a reward system such as a sticker chart for listening to instructions, for concentrating and for finishing the activity.

Here are some tips for coping with overactivity:

- Organise your day so there are Active Times and Quiet Times. Build Quiet Times into daily routines, such as before bed and after lunch. Remember that you still need to keep an eye on your child whatever he is doing; don't expect him to get on with it by himself.
- Give your child opportunities to be active and run around freely. Best not just before bedtime!
- Set up a reward chart for being quiet during Quiet Times. You can encourage your child to choose to listen to a story, play with a puzzle, look at a picture book or just have a little rest. (At school, your child will need to be able to sit quietly on a mat for story-time and not be running around the classroom.)

What If the Action Plans Haven't Worked?

If you have tried to follow an Action Plan closely over a period of several months and your child's concentration is still not improving, you may have to take further action. A very small number of children have severe attention deficit problems. If this seems to be the case for your child, you should consider seeking professional help. You will need to go to your GP to obtain a referral to a paediatrician at a hospital or clinic.

TOP TIP: Encourage your child to focus on a structured activity for a short time every day – reward him for working nicely and finishing it.

Prepare for Reading

The building blocks for reading are developed in the pre-school years. These consist of *foundation skills* and *specific pre-reading skills*. You as a parent can do a lot to ensure that these are in place for day one of your child's school life.

Foundation Skills

The foundation skills relevant for reading are:

- Building up a spoken vocabulary.
- Developing listening comprehension.

- Enjoyment at looking through books and listening to stories.
- Understanding concepts of print (such as what letters are, what words are, where the top of the page is, in which direction we read, that is, from left to right).

Check to see if your child has these foundation skills by answering the following questions:

Ready to Read Questionnaire

1. Spoken Vocabulary and Listening Comprehension   Yes   No

Does your child point to pictures in books and name them? ☐ ☐

Will your child name an object pictured in a book when you point? For instance, if you say 'What's that?', will she tell you what the picture is of? ☐ ☐

Can your child describe in her own words the story sequence in a picture book as you go from page to page? For instance, you might ask her: 'What happened to the children after they set off to the shops?' ☐ ☐

	Yes	No
Can your child remember or 'fill in' some words or phrases from familiar books? If you said, for instance, 'And then they all went to the ....' could she fill in the correct word from her knowledge of the story?	☐	☐

2. Awareness and Enjoyment of Books

Does your child:

	Yes	No
Enjoy listening to you read a short story?	☐	☐
Look at picture books and story books for herself?	☐	☐
Like to listen to story tapes?	☐	☐
Talk with you about what's happening in the story while you're reading it?	☐	☐
Have favourite books she asks you to read to her?	☐	☐
Attempt to 'mimic' reading? For instance, 'reading' a book to her teddy bear?	☐	☐

3. Concepts of Print

Does your child know:

	Yes	No
How to hold a book correctly?	☐	☐
That print is different from pictures?	☐	☐
Which the title page is?	☐	☐

	Yes	No
Where the front of the book is?	☐	☐
Where the back of the book is?	☐	☐
Where the top of the page is?	☐	☐
Where the bottom of the page is?	☐	☐
To turn the pages at the right time and in the right direction?	☐	☐
That the pictures relate to the text? (Does she point to the pictures as you read?)	☐	☐
That we read from left to right?	☐	☐
That each printed word corresponds to a spoken word? (Can she point to words as you speak them?)	☐	☐

If you answered 'yes' to many of the questions, then your child is well prepared to move on to the specific pre-reading skills (see page 124).

If you answered 'no' to quite a few of the questions, take note of these areas and work on them, following the tips below.

Here are some tips for linking spoken vocabulary to print:

- Use the pictures in books to help your child develop her vocabulary. Ask her, 'What is that a picture of?', 'What's the girl holding?'
- If your child doesn't know a word, talk to her about it in simple language – maybe you could draw a picture together that shows its meaning.
- Keep your definitions of words simple and child-friendly, perhaps using a gesture or an example if needed.
- When you and your child come across the 'new' word for a second or third time, draw her attention to it again and ask her if she remembers what it means.

Your child needs good listening comprehension so she can understand what the teacher is saying, and it is important for later reading comprehension too. Use the shared reading experience to help your child develop listening comprehension. Here are some tips for developing listening comprehension:

- Ask her to tell back to you what happened on a given page of the story. Begin by letting her look at the picture (as a prompt), but later on, turn the page over and ask her to describe what has just happened (when she doesn't have a picture in front of her to help).

- Ask her specific questions about what happened in the story, such as, 'Can you remember what was special about Jenny's magic hat?', 'Why is the cat hiding in the toy box?'
- Ask her to tell the whole story back to you. Say to her, 'Can you tell me the story now?' She can look at the pictures in the book as prompts (together with occasional 'cue' questions from you) while she is telling you the story.
- Help her to draw conclusions by making inferences. This means going beyond what is specifically described in the story and working out what might happen next or how people might be feeling. For example, 'How do you think Jenny felt when she saw that her mummy was cross with her?'

Here are some tips for improving book, story and print awareness:

- Choose short books that can easily be read in one sitting; the print should be large and well spaced with simple sentences.

- Ideally, read the book yourself before reading it to your child – you can then plan ahead how you want to present certain sections of the story.

- Before starting to read the story, look together at the cover, read the title and the author's (and maybe the illustrator's) name.

- Say something brief about what the book is about.

- Turn to the first page and say, 'This is the beginning of our story,' and when you reach the last page, close the book and say, 'That's the end of our story.'

- Every so often, stop to make a comment or ask a question: 'What do you think Jenny will do next?'

- Give your child experience of handling the book by letting her hold it some of the time, and encourage her to turn the pages.

- Point under the words with your finger and glide your finger along the line as you read.

- Encourage your child to join in rhymes or repetitive phrases, or to fill in missing words in familiar books.

Specific Pre-Reading Skills

For children to begin to make sense of print, just two very specific skills need to be in place: awareness that words are made up of sounds – *phonological awareness* – and *knowing the alphabet letters*.

Phonological awareness means children's realisation that the spoken words they hear and use are made up of sequences of sounds. The main sets of sounds in words are **syllables** and **phonemes**.

Syllables are units in a word that consist of a vowel with one or two consonants on either side. For instance, in the word 'carpet' there are two syllables: 'car' and 'pet'. Syllables may be more easily understood by your child if you explain to her that they are about listening to the 'beats' in the word; you could tap on the table or clap your hands while you beat three times for the word 'bu-tter-fly'.

Phonemes are the smallest units of speech sounds. It is important not to confuse phonemes with letters. While there are three phonemes in the three-letter word 'dog' ('d', 'o' and 'g'), there are also three phonemes in the four-letter word 'chin' ('ch', 'i' and 'n') because 'ch' makes one speech sound. Similarly, in the five-letter word 'sheep', there are also just three phonemes ('sh', 'ee' and 'p') because 'sh' and 'ee' both make only one sound.

Pronouncing Sounds (Phonemes)

When working with phonemes, it is important to pronounce the consonants as clearly as possible. When pronouncing 'b' and 'm', for example, be careful not to add an 'uh', like 'buh' or 'muh'; this 'uh' sound is called a 'schwa' – it does tend to distort sounds, so keep it to a minimum. Pronouncing the schwa risks turning a word like 'dog' into something like 'duh-o-guh'. The letters 'd' and 'g' need to be pronounced with very short, sharp sounds as they actually sound in the word – 'dd' and 'gg'. The same is true for all the other consonants – 'bb', 'mm', 'ss', and so on – to cut out the schwa.

Check Your Child's Awareness of Words and Sounds and her Letter Knowledge

Beginning, Middle and End Words

Does your child understand what are the beginning, middle and end words in a short sentence? Ask her:

		Yes	No
What is the **beginning** word in:	*My* red book.	☐	☐
What is the **middle** word in:	I *like* chocolate.	☐	☐
What is the **end** word in:	Time to *play*.	☐	☐

Awareness of Syllables

Is your child able to *beat out* the syllables in a word, by clapping them as she says them (or tapping on a table if she'd prefer)? Ask her to clap (or tap) with a beat the syllables in her own name and your name, before trying two-syllable words like (the answers are given in brackets):

	Yes	No
flower (beat-beat)	☐	☐
story (beat-beat)	☐	☐
picture (beat-beat)	☐	☐

Is your child able to *blend* (or join) syllables to make words? Say a two-syllable word, pausing for about a second between the syllables, and ask her, 'What word am I saying?'

	Yes	No
rain-bow (rainbow)	☐	☐
pen-guin (penguin)	☐	☐
chil-dren (children)	☐	☐

Maybe try some longer words that have three syllables:

	Yes	No
el-e-phant (elephant)	☐	☐
re-mem-ber (remember)	☐	☐
di-no-saur (dinosaur)	☐	☐

Is your child able to *segment* (or break) words into syllables? Can she say what the **beginning** beat (syllable) is in:

	Yes	No
carpet (car)	☐	☐
donkey (don)	☐	☐
spider (spy)	☐	☐

Can she say what the **end** beat (syllable) is in:

	Yes	No
window (dow)	☐	☐

	Yes	No
postman (man)	☐	☐
snowdrop (drop)	☐	☐

Rhyming

Can your child finish off a nursery rhyme that you've started?

	Yes	No
Hickory dickory dock, the mouse ran up the … (clock)	☐	☐
Jack and Jill went up the … (hill)	☐	☐
Can she tell you words she knows that rhyme with **fan**?	☐	☐

Give her an example like 'tan'. Can she think of any others? Make a note of the rhyming words that she says (even nonsense words like 'zan' and 'gan' are acceptable as long as they rhyme).

Awareness of Phonemes

Can your child *blend* two or three sounds together to make a word? Make sure you say the *sound* (not the *name*) of each letter (*before you do this check, see page 125 on pronouncing sounds correctly*). Say each phoneme in the word with a one-second pause between each. Ask your child, 'What word am I saying?'

	Yes	No
s-o (so)	☐	☐
i-s (is)	☐	☐
t-ea (tea)	☐	☐
d-a-d (dad)	☐	☐
p-i-g (pig)	☐	☐
Can your child play 'I Spy'?	☐	☐

Say, 'I spy with my little eye some things that begin with "f". Can you find them?' Your child may say, 'Flower, floor, finger', etc. Now try another sound, say 't' (for 'table, toy, teddy').

'I Spy' leads to working on the segmentation check below because you are drawing your child's attention to the idea of 'beginning with' or 'first', which some four-year-olds can find a little hard.

Can your child *segment* (or break) words into phonemes? Can she say what the **first** sound is in the words:

		Yes	No
cat	'c'	☐	☐
pig	'p'	☐	☐
top	't'	☐	☐

Can she say what the **end** sound is in the words:

		Yes	No
cat	't'	☐	☐
pig	'g'	☐	☐
top	'p'	☐	☐

Letter Knowledge

How many letters of the alphabet does your child know? Ask her 'What do these letters say?' Tick off each letter correctly identified, whether your child gives the name or the sound.

s m f t g q

a l o r z p

i y b h k e

w c j n d v

x u

If you've answered 'yes' to many of the questions, your child clearly has very good phonological awareness and is well prepared to get to grips with reading after she starts school. If you've recorded quite a few 'no's', don't worry. It is not unusual for pre-school children to have difficulty with some of these skills. Below are some games and activities that will help your child build up her phonological awareness ready for school. If your child knows around half the letters of the alphabet, that's fine. If she knows fewer than this, it would be a good idea to start building up her letter knowledge before she starts school.

Here are some tips for building awareness of words, syllables and sounds:

1. Learn about beginning, middle and end

You will have realised from the check whether your child understands the meaning of these important words – beginning, middle and end. If she seems unsure, give her some practice in showing you which is the beginning, the middle and the end in a series of three. You could use almost anything for this practice: try with counters or pictures. Say to your child, 'Point to the beginning picture, now to the end picture, and now to the middle picture.'

2. Learn about words in sentences

Get her to beat or clap the words she hears in a sentence: so two claps for 'Bobby runs', three claps for 'Jenny is happy', four claps for 'My dog is big.' Encourage her to clap each word as she says it.

3. Learn about syllables

● Beat out syllables in words. You could get your child to clap the syllables she hears (or even says herself) in a two- or three-syllable word (see below).

You say: 'pencil', then 'pen-cil'
Child says: 'pencil' while going clap clap

You say: 'elephant', then 'el-e-phant'
Child says: 'elephant' while going clap clap clap

● Practise blending syllables to make words. You could use a puppet or doll for this. Explain to your child that the doll says words very slowly. Ask your child what word the doll is trying to say. Start with two-syllable words like 'car-pet', 'bis-cuit', 'par-ty', 'pic-ture', saying the word with a short pause (around a second) between the two syllables. Once your child is good at this, move on to three-syllable words like 'di-no-saur', 'bu-tter-fly', 'al-pha-bet', and eventually four-syllable words like 'a-lli-ga-tor', 'ca-ter-pill-ar'.

- See if your child can tell you which is the beginning syllable in words like 'car-pet', 'don-key', 'trac-tor', and which is the end syllable in 'car-pet', 'don-key', 'trac-tor'.

- See if your child can finish off the second syllable in a two-syllable word. Gather together some pictures of objects with two-syllable names like 'apple', 'monkey', 'circle'. Show your child the picture of each of these and say, 'I'm going to say the beginning of the word – you finish it off for me. Here is a "cir-",' to which your child should respond '-cle'.

- Get your child to take away a syllable from a two-syllable word. You'd say, 'What's carpet without saying "car"?' (answer: 'pet'); 'What's "dinner" without saying "din"?' (answer: 'er').

4. Learn about rhyming

- Recite nursery rhymes together; read books that have rhyming verses; make up silly rhymes; ask your child to finish off the last word in a sentence from a familiar nursery rhyme, such as 'Hickory, dickory, dock, the mouse ran up the ...?' (answer: 'clock').
- Together, think up words that rhyme with each other.

Here are some examples:

Which words rhyme with...?

lid	**mat**	**rug**	**pot**	**pen**
kid	pat	dug	hot	ten
did	sat	mug	dot	hen
rid	hat	jug	cot	den
bid	rat	tug	lot	men

And what about some silly words?

fid	lat	wug	zot	ren
nid	jat	zug	fot	nen
pid	wat	gug	vot	sen

● Help your child find rhyming words by showing her a picture of, say, a cat. You say, 'Here's a cat. I'm going to say two more words. Which of them rhymes with cat?' Then say, clearly and slowly, 'pat, bag'. Your child needs to pick out which is the word that rhymes (in this case 'pat').

Here are a few more examples:

Star:	**jar**	pat
Face:	late	**race**
Box:	**fox**	pot

5. Learn about speech sounds (phonemes)

Awareness of phonemes begins in the pre-school years, but only at a fairly basic level. This skill continues to develop during the first year at school as your child builds up her reading vocabulary. The activities suggested here concentrate only on phoneme awareness skills that your child needs for starting school.

● Practise blending speech sounds. This is a fairly easy task even for four- to five-year-olds. Keep the words nice and short, and no longer than two or three phonemes. Say to your child, 'What word do these sounds make: s-ee, i-s, a-t, g-o?', and then later three-phoneme words like 'd-o-g', 'p-i-ck', 'd-a-d', 'sh-i-p'.

- Practise identifying phonemes. See if your child can tell which is the beginning, middle and end phoneme in simple three-phoneme words like 'd-o-g', 'sh-i-p' and 'c-a-t'.

- Get your child to clap the phonemes she hears you say – two claps for 'go', 'see' and 'at', and three claps for 'dog', 'dad' and 'fish'.

- Ask your child to think of words that begin with the same sound. This is called **alliteration**. Say to her, 'I'm going to say a word that begins with the "s" sound – "sun". Let's try and think of some others. What about "sad"? Can you think of some more?' She may come up with 'sip', 'stick', 'sorry', 'sandwich', 'sock'. Then you say, 'Shall we make up some silly words that begin with "s"? What about "sut"? Can you think of some?' Your child may come up with silly words that you can laugh at together like 'saf', 'sog', 'sul'.

Here are some more examples of alliteration:

Can you think of words that begin with the sound:				
	f	t	p	m	c
Your example	*fun*	*tin*	*pat*	*mug*	*cap*
Your child	fat	tag	pot	mine	cot
might say	furry	tiger	pink	mat	can
	fireman	tummy	pretty	middle	cut
	fizzy	tomorrow	pattern	money	cup

● Get your child to **finish off** phonemes in words. Show her pictures of things that have a single-syllable name, like 'cat'. Tell her you're going to say the first part of the word 'ca' and you'd like her to finish it off. So, she says 't'.

Play Games to Help Your Child Learn Some Letters of the Alphabet

The current practice in the UK is to teach letter sounds before letter names. Like most adults, you may be more comfortable with letter names, but if your child's school teaches letter sounds first, you will need to check how to pronounce the sounds correctly (see page 125).

Letters are not usually taught in alphabetical order, 'a' through to 'z', but by how common the letters are in words. Therefore, you might begin with six letter sounds that let you make up many three-letter words:

s a t i p n

Once your child has learned these six letter sounds, she has the basis for beginning to learn to read simple words like 'sat', 'pit', 'tan', 'tip', 'pan', 'sip' and so on.

The next set of consonants your child might learn could be:

d g h k alongside another vowel, e

Much later on (most likely at school), your child will learn the least commonly used letters, like:

q z w v together with the vowels, o and u

If you're teaching letter names first, your child will find it easier to learn the names of letters that are very close to the sounds they represent. Therefore, learning letters like y, w, h is harder and may take longer than learning letters like s, b, t and so on. This is because for the letter s, the sound 'ss' sounds very similar to the name 'es'. However, for the letter w, the sound 'ww' sounds very different to the name, 'double-u'.

Here are some tips for collecting material useful for learning letters:

- Get colourful alphabet books.
- Collect DVDs or videos that include alphabet games.
- Buy a set of plastic or felt letters (in lower case) or make yourself a little pack of cards with a letter of the alphabet written in large lower-case lettering on each.
- Make a collection of objects that begin with the letters of the alphabet you're working on with your child. You could use a plastic cow to represent the letter c. Use objects that begin with the usual beginning sound for the letter; so a sock to represent the letter s, but not a shoe because its beginning sound is 'sh'.
- Also, make a collection of pictures of everyday objects beginning with the different alphabet letters.

Here are some tips for learning letters:

- Play games with the letters, objects and pictures you have collected. These work for letter sounds and for letter names.
- Sort into little piles objects or pictures that begin with the same letter. For instance, when you're working on the letter c, pick out from your picture stack images of a cat, a cup, a clock and so on. After the pictures have been grouped together, put your plastic letter 'c' next to it and say, 'Here is the letter c; "c" for cat.'
- Use the pictures you've collected to help your child make her own alphabet book. Use one page for each letter, write it in large lower-case print at the top and then stick the pictures in place under the letter.
- Play 'I Spy' with the objects or pictures, together with the alphabet letters you've been working on.

Specific Learning Difficulties

The term *specific learning difficulty* is used when a child has a problem in learning a particular skill, in contrast to her other abilities which appear to be developing well. Children with specific learning difficulties may be very bright. In cases of dyslexia, for example, which affects reading ability, it is not unusual for children to be doing very well in other aspects of their learning.

Because so many children find it hard to learn to read, there has been a lot of research into how to assess and help children with dyslexia. We now know what puts children 'at risk' for dyslexia, even in the pre-school years. To check, are any of the following relevant to your child?

- Is there a family history of poor reading and spelling?
- Was your child late to talk, or does she have unclear speech that other people find hard to follow?
- Has your child found it hard to learn nursery rhymes or to play 'I Spy'?
- Is your child finding it hard to learn and remember the letters of the alphabet?

If you have answered 'yes' to at least two out of the four questions, your child is at risk for reading difficulties. Dyslexia is commonly inherited and many children with dyslexia have had early speech and language problems.

Here are some tips for what to do:

- Keep up the activities to help your child with print aware-ness, phonological awareness and alphabet learning, as described above. Working on sounds in words and on letters is the best preventive action you can take (along with reading books to, and with, your child).
- Take it slowly, and make sure your child can do the simpler activities before you move on to the harder ones.
- Remember to make the activities enjoyable for your child – keep it relaxed, make it fun, and if you are anxious about your child struggling, don't show it!
- Let your child's future school know your concerns.

If your child has difficulties that persist into her second year at school, it will be important to arrange for her to have an assess-ment with a specialist literacy teacher or psychologist.

★ **TOP TIP:** Read, read, read with your child. Enjoy lots of books and stories together and play fun sound and letter games.

9

Prepare for Number Work

Children begin to develop an awareness of numbers from a remarkably early age. You and your child can together work on the early *concrete* number skills. He will then be well prepared for learning about *abstract* maths when he starts school.

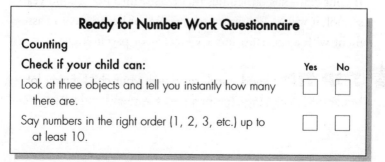

Ready for Number Work Questionnaire		
Counting		
Check if your child can:	Yes	No
Look at three objects and tell you instantly how many there are.	☐	☐
Say numbers in the right order (1, 2, 3, etc.) up to at least 10.	☐	☐

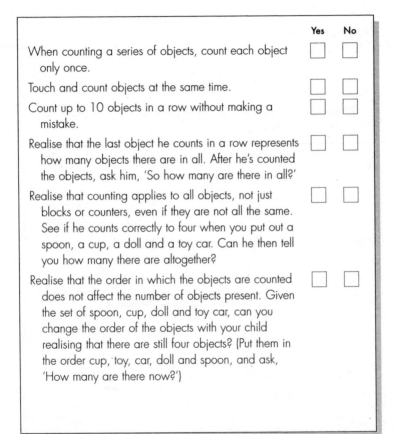

	Yes	No
When counting a series of objects, count each object only once.	☐	☐
Touch and count objects at the same time.	☐	☐
Count up to 10 objects in a row without making a mistake.	☐	☐
Realise that the last object he counts in a row represents how many objects there are in all. After he's counted the objects, ask him, 'So how many are there in all?'	☐	☐
Realise that counting applies to all objects, not just blocks or counters, even if they are not all the same. See if he counts correctly to four when you put out a spoon, a cup, a doll and a toy car. Can he then tell you how many there are altogether?	☐	☐
Realise that the order in which the objects are counted does not affect the number of objects present. Given the set of spoon, cup, doll and toy car, can you change the order of the objects with your child realising that there are still four objects? (Put them in the order cup, toy, car, doll and spoon, and ask, 'How many are there now?')	☐	☐

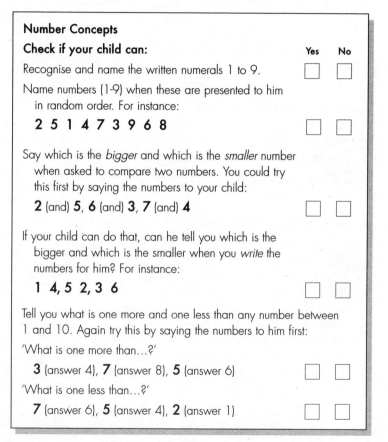

Number Concepts

Check if your child can:

	Yes	No

Recognise and name the written numerals 1 to 9.

Name numbers (1-9) when these are presented to him in random order. For instance:

2 5 1 4 7 3 9 6 8

Say which is the *bigger* and which is the *smaller* number when asked to compare two numbers. You could try this first by saying the numbers to your child:

2 (and) **5**, **6** (and) **3**, **7** (and) **4**

If your child can do that, can he tell you which is the bigger and which is the smaller when you *write* the numbers for him? For instance:

1 4, 5 2, 3 6

Tell you what is one more and one less than any number between 1 and 10. Again try this by saying the numbers to him first:

'What is one more than…?'

3 (answer 4), **7** (answer 8), **5** (answer 6)

'What is one less than…?'

7 (answer 6), **5** (answer 4), **2** (answer 1)

	Yes	No
If your child can do this quite easily, now *show* him the numbers.		
'What is one more than…?'		
4 (answer 5), **6** (answer 7), **2** (answer 3)	☐	☐
'What is one less than…?'		
7 (answer 6), **2** (answer 1), **9** (answer 8)	☐	☐

Do addition and subtraction with very small numbers (up to around 5) using his fingers or by counting in his head if he can. Ask him questions like:

'Susan has two blocks and Mummy gives her one more – how many blocks will she have altogether?' (answer: 3) ☐ ☐

'Danny has four toy cars and he loses two of them – how many will he have left?' (answer: 2) ☐ ☐

Show some ability to write down numbers. For instance, if you show your child three counters, can he represent them either by drawing three circles or by drawing 'tally marks' to represent them (| | |) or even writing the number itself (3)? ☐ ☐

Patterns

Check if your child can:

	Yes	No

Copy a sequence of objects you've set up for him, using, e.g., beads of different colours or shapes. ☐ ☐

For instance:

Continue (or keep going) a pattern or sequence you've started for him – for instance, like the one above. ☐ ☐

Set up a pattern of his own and then continue it. ☐ ☐

Shape and Space

Check if your child can:

	Yes	No

Recognise and *name* **lines**, **squares**, **circles** and **triangles** when these are shown to him. ☐ ☐

Sort objects according to **colour**, **shape** and **size** (so all the blue items are in one group, the red in another; and, similarly, the big objects are in one group and the small objects in the other). ☐ ☐

	Yes	No
Match objects by **colour, size** or **shape**; for instance, showing your child a blue object then asking him to choose an object of the same colour from a group of objects of different colours.	☐	☐
Use differently shaped objects to *create patterns* or other objects, such as putting triangles, squares or rectangles together to make a house.	☐	☐

Measurement
Check if your child can:

	Yes	No
Say which line is longest and which is shortest in the following.	☐	☐

———————————

——————————————————

————————

| Say which is the heavier or lighter of two objects you ask him to hold. | ☐ | ☐ |
| Order three objects according to length from shortest to longest, for example, these lines: | ☐ | ☐ |

———————————————

——————————

—————————————————

This becomes

_____

followed by

_____

and finally

_____

If you have answered 'yes' to most of the above questions, your child is clearly well prepared for learning about abstract maths at school.

If you have answered 'no' to many or even a few then it would be helpful to focus on developing these less secure skills.

Learn to Count

There are five concepts that children need to get to grips with before they can be said to be counting. These are:

1 *The one-to-one principle*. This means that children match the counting words they're saying to the items they're

counting. To understand this principle, children have first to be able to recite the counting words in order: 1, 2, 3, 4 and so on. Second, they need to touch and count each object only once; you may have noticed that when your child was first learning to count, he often touched an object more than once, so counting it again. Finally, the child needs to count the number (best out loud to start with) at the same time as touching the object.

2 *The stable order principle.* This is the child's realisation that the order of counting words is always the same: we count 1, 2, 3, never 2, 1, 3.

3 *The cardinal principle.* The final number in any count represents how many are in the set or group. The child must therefore be able to stop on the last number of the count and recognise that number as how many there are altogether. If he counts three blocks, he says, '1, 2, 3,' and can then say, 'There are three blocks.'

4 *The abstraction principle* means that counting can be applied to any set of objects, whether they are all the same (such as four blue blocks) or different objects (such as a block, a doll, a toy car, a hairbrush). It is not until children

are around five that they understand that they can count different objects in the same group.

5 *The order irrelevance principle* is children's understanding that the order in which objects are counted does not affect the number. For instance, in a set consisting of a block, a doll, a toy car and a hairbrush, it is perfectly all right to call the block 'one' the first time he counts them and the doll 'one' the second time he counts them.

To become successful at counting, your child needs opportunities to:

● Use language of quantity to make comparisons between objects; in particular, he needs to learn words like more, less, the same, and so on.
● Recite the number names so he becomes consistent in this.
● Count out a given quantity of items; for instance, give your child 10 blocks and ask him to count out six of them.
● Count items in a set (see below).

Here are some tips for developing counting skills:

● Use common objects, dolls' house furniture, small toys

and pictures to develop your child's understanding of 'more', 'less', 'same', etc. You can put out toy animals in a field and then ask your child questions like:

- 'Can you put **all** the cows in the field?'
- 'Can you put just a **few** pigs in the field?'
- 'Are there **more** pigs or **more** cows in the field?'
- 'Let's take some pigs out of the field – can you take the **same** number of cows out of the field?'

● Recite numbers in the right order.
  - Make lots of opportunities for counting, whether you are reciting number songs and rhymes, counting children at a party, counting candles on a birthday cake and so on. This helps your child realise that the order of numbers is always the same.

● Count out a given quantity.
  - Ask your child to put, for example, four spoons on the table for tea, or put six toy cows in the field, give you four of the coins he's holding, put two spoons of sugar in Mummy's teacup.

● Count items in a set. Lots of materials can be used for counting, including blocks, toy cars, shells and pebbles, coins, beads, objects within a picture. Give your child the opportunity to:

- Count objects that can be moved – that is, get him to move the objects to one side as he counts them.
- Count a mixed set of objects more than once, with the objects in a different order each time.
- Count objects that can be touched but not moved, such as objects shown within a picture.
- Count sounds such as taps on a table, musical sounds made by a drum or trumpet, words in a little sentence you say to him.
- Count physical movements like claps, hops and steps.

● Make or buy a number frieze that shows the link between the written number and the number of objects, e.g. the number 3 and three smiley faces ☺ ☺ ☺

Learn to Add and Take Away

Play 'one more/one less' games, either using objects like blocks, or fingers. For example:

- 'Here are two blocks. Here's one more. Now there are ...?' (answer: 3).
- 'Show me four fingers. Put one finger down. How many are there now?' (answer: 3).
- 'Put four biscuits on the plate. Now put another biscuit on the plate. How many are there altogether?' (answer: 5).
- 'Put three biscuits on the plate. Why don't you eat one biscuit? How many are there now?' (answer: 2).
- 'Here are six blocks. Let's take one away. How many are left?' (answer: 5).

Learn About Patterns

Children learn about ordering at a very young age in all sorts of play situations. Even two-year-olds love lining up objects like toy cars, dolls or blocks. As they get older, they begin to order their toys to form patterns. They might string beads together in alternating colours (red-blue-red-blue), line up bricks in alternating sizes (big-little-big-little), or put shapes into sequences like circle-square-triangle, circle-square-triangle. Ask your child questions like, 'What comes first?', 'What comes next?', 'Tell me about the pattern you've made.' This draws his attention to the order of the objects and makes him understand what a sequence is.

Once your child is happily copying and repeating patterns you set for him, see if he can create a pattern of his own. This is important not just to show that he too can make a sequence, but it helps develop his creativity as well.

Learn About Shapes and Space

One of the first and most important ways children come to understand shapes is through using language to describe the properties of each shape.

Here are some tips for helping your child to describe and sort objects:

- Use words describing texture – like 'rough', 'smooth', 'hard', 'soft', 'fluffy', 'sharp'.
- Teach colour – use the proper names to describe the colour of objects and practise sorting by colour.
- Play with shapes – sort kitchen objects into things that are

round and curvy such as jars, pans, bowls and plates, and things that are straight such as knives and forks.

- Draw and talk about lines – straight or curvy, long or short, thick or thin.
- Point out size – describe objects as 'big', 'small', 'fat', 'thin' and sort them into groups of big or small, fat or thin objects.

Introduce your child to jigsaws and puzzles. Start with simple ones before moving on to harder ones that involve putting more pieces together. Talk your child through his actions, saying things like, 'Where will this piece fit?', 'Do you think you might need to turn that piece round to fit it in?'

Here are some tips for activities with 2-D shapes:

- Sort different size shapes into groups of triangles, squares and circles.

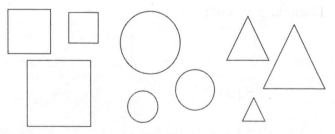

● Ask your child to copy-draw these shapes:

Mummy's turn:

Child's turn:

● Learn the names of the shapes:

Square **Circle** **Triangle**

- Combine shapes to make patterns or objects like faces, houses, people and cars:

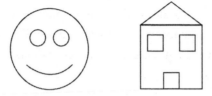

Learn About Measurement

Measurement is a very important life skill. Pre-schoolers have the opportunity to make lots of measurement decisions – who has the biggest teddy, who got the smaller piece of cake (they can be very good at this one!), how tall they are in relation to their nursery classmates.

Here are some useful words to use with your child when you play measurement games together:

- *Length* – talk about 'long', 'tall', 'short', 'little'. Gather together objects (toys or just household materials) that vary in size and use these words to describe them.

- *Weight* – in addition to using the words 'heavy' and 'light', use the verb 'weigh'; for instance, 'Shall we weigh this box on our kitchen scales and see how heavy it is?'
- *Capacity* – talk about containers that are filled with liquid, sand, coloured balls, etc. Describe containers as either 'full' or 'empty'.
- *Volume* – use words like 'big', 'little', 'small', 'thick', 'wide', 'thin'.

Encourage children to make comparisons and to develop the vocabulary of comparison. This includes words like 'bigger', 'shorter', 'heavier', 'highest', 'thinner', 'less', 'more'.

Another aspect of measurement is time. Use daily routines to introduce your child to the language of time, using words such as 'morning', 'afternoon', 'bedtime', 'before', 'after', 'then', 'now', 'next'. Talk about past events – what he did that morning at nursery; where he went last weekend. Talk about his next birthday, or a special outing or holiday that's coming up. Use words such as 'tomorrow', 'soon', 'next week', 'next month'.

A final measurement concept you can introduce your child

to at the pre-school stage is speed. Talk about how long an activity or event takes. Use words like 'slowly', 'quickly', 'fast', 'start', 'stop'. Again, it is useful to make comparisons. Ask your child to:

- Walk slowly.
- Now speed up and walk quickly.
- Now run so you move faster.
- Now stop.
- Now start (again) and run as fast as you can.

Problems with Number Work

There is evidence that certain number skills allow us to predict at the pre-school stage how easily children will learn maths when they start school. Ask yourself the following questions:

- Can your child count up to 10 objects in a row without making a mistake?
- Can your child compare two numbers and say which is the bigger and which is the smaller?
- Can your child subitise (look at between two and four

objects and say *quickly* how many there are without actually counting them)? Try it with the dots below:

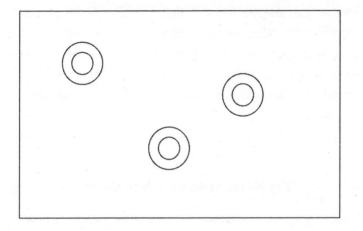

If your child has difficulty with any of these, he may be 'at risk' for later maths problems. However, don't be alarmed. Keep practising and, when your child has started school, talk to his teacher about your concerns and, together, keep an eye on his progress.

⭐ **TOP TIP:** Opportunities for learning about numbers, shapes, patterns and measurement are around us all the time, whether out shopping (for example, counting the change), measuring ingredients when cooking, sorting clothes items for the washing machine, setting the table, measuring a child's height and so on. You can use these day-to-day activities in a fun way to help develop your child's awareness of numbers.

10

Prepare for Writing

While you are teaching your child about letters, sounds and reading, you can begin to look at writing letters too.

Is Your Child Ready to Write?

Work through the following questionnaire to see whether your child is ready to learn to write some letters.

Letter Writing Questionnaire

	Yes	No
Has your child decided which hand to use for writing?	☐	☐
Does your child hold the pencil correctly most of the time? (see page 167)	☐	☐
Does your child enjoy painting pictures with colours and a paintbrush?	☐	☐
Can your child colour in large shapes with different-coloured crayons and (mostly) stay within the lines?	☐	☐
Does your child draw pictures of people, houses, animals, etc., that are recognisable?	☐	☐
Can your child use stencils for making shapes and pictures (with maybe a little help from you to hold the stencil)?	☐	☐

Can your child copy-draw the following shapes?

Shapes   **Child's Turn**

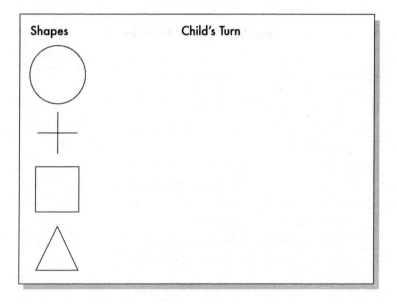

Shapes　　　　　　　　　　**Child's Turn**

If you answered 'yes' to the above questions, your child is ready to start to learn to write.

If you have answered 'no' to quite a few of the questions, it would be a good idea to hold off teaching your child how to write letters for the moment while you concentrate on some of the basic skills covered in the questionnaire.

Being Right- or Left-Handed

By the age of five, 90 per cent of children will clearly prefer to use either the right or left hand for most hand actions. However, it is not unusual for a child who writes with her right hand to show a preference for unscrewing a jar with her left. This is nothing to worry about – let your child decide which hand to use.

If, however, your child shows no preference for drawing or writing with one hand or the other by around four-and-a-half, this may be a warning sign of problems to come. Give your child lots of opportunities for drawing and painting and talk to your child's teacher about your concerns so that you can work together and watch over her progress.

Learn to Hold the Pencil Correctly

Between the ages of three and five, children start using the correct pencil grip that involves just one finger on the top of the pencil – so the pencil is held between the thumb and the index finger.

The diagram below shows what the correct grip should be for both right- and left-handers.

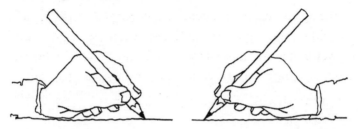

Probably the easiest way to encourage your child to hold the pencil correctly is to use one of the triangular-shaped rubber pencil grips you can buy through educational suppliers or at educational bookshops.

Here are some tips to help your child develop the motor and spatial skills needed for writing. Encourage your child to:

- Paint with a brush and easel to help develop gross motor (large movement) skills.
- Colour in pictures to practise pencil grip and fine up-and-down and side-to-side movements (fine motor skills) needed for writing.

- Trace over pre-drawn lines or dotted lines of different kinds (horizontal, vertical, zigzag, curved, circular).
- Do pencil and paper 'dot-to-dot' picture puzzles, draw the way out of mazes, play pegboard pattern games, string beads, and use lacing and sewing cards.
- Do jigsaw puzzles, build with Lego, stack blocks and make block patterns, match shapes and pictures.
- Draw pictures of favourite objects and scenes.
- Draw repeating patterns – see if your child can copy-draw (or trace with her finger in sand, flour or glitter) and then 'keep going' the following sequences:

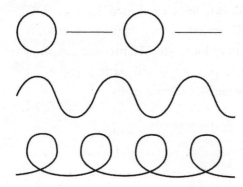

Begin to Write Letters

Once your child is comfortable with these pre-writing activities, she should be ready to learn how to write some letters. However, before you start teaching your child to write letters, here are some important tips:

● Get the posture right – it's best for your child to write while seated at a proper table, not while lying on the floor or at a coffee table. Use a straight-backed chair, make sure her feet are comfortably on the ground and that the table is at a suitable height.

● Get the paper in the right position – the position of the paper in relation to the pencil is important, particularly for left-handers. If your child is left-handed, the paper should be angled to the left so your child can easily see what she's writing. This means she can avoid an uncomfortable curved 'hook' position – and she will be less likely to smudge her work.

● Get the language right – practise words that describe letters and their position on the page. Does your child know what the letter *before*, the letter *after* and the letter *next to* mean? Show her a sequence of letters (or even shapes if you like) and ask her which comes before, which comes after and which letters are next to a given letter.

For example, in the letter sequence:

f t a g m

ask your child, 'Which letter is before "a"?' (she should respond 't'); 'Which letter is after "a"?' (she should respond 'g'); 'Which letters are next to "a"?' (she should respond 't' and 'g').

'Big' or 'little' letters?

Children usually learn lower-case letters before upper case. In the year before your child starts school, concentrate on lower case – maybe leave the upper-case letters for her to learn after she's started school. Don't feel under pressure to teach all 26 letters during the pre-school years. It's a good idea, though, for your child to learn how to write her first name and maybe a few more letters besides.

Here are some tips for the early stages of writing letters:

- Start with matching games. Make up two sets of the letters in your child's name on individual cards, with one letter per card. Put these on the table in front of her (not necessarily in the right order). Now give her the second set of cards and see if she can match the letters.

- Help your child understand how letters relate to lines on a page by first drawing a thick line on a blank sheet of paper. Now see if your child can place wooden or plastic alphabet letters on this line so they are correctly positioned. Below is how they should be positioned for all the letters of the alphabet:

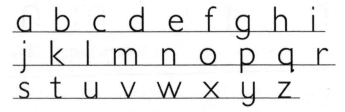

- Write the letters in the air using big arm movements, while saying the sound (or name) of the letter as you're 'writing it'. Make sure you start the letter in the right place (see opposite). Remember to say the sound correctly. (Pronunciation of sounds is covered on page 125.) You may need to guide your child's hand to begin with until she gets the idea of copying you, and before she can do it on her own.

- Write large letters with a thick marker pen on pieces of coloured cardboard, squeeze glue over the outline of the letters, and then sprinkle on salt, glitter or sand and let it dry. Mark the starting position of the letter with a coloured dot.

a b c d e f g
h i j k l m n
o p q r s t u
v w x y z

Starting at the dot, get your child to trace over the letter with her index finger while saying its name or sound out loud. Again, you may need to guide her hand to begin with, before she can manage the tracing on her own.

- Get some stencils of letters (and maybe numbers too) and have your child draw inside the boundaries.

Problems With Writing

If, by the time your child starts school, she has learned how to:

- hold a pencil correctly
- write her first name from memory
- write around half the letters of the alphabet from memory
- write a few simple and favourite words
- write most of the letters fairly evenly and legibly

she will be very well prepared for writing at school. But what if your child has problems? Some children take to drawing and writing very easily and naturally. Others seem to find it much more difficult.

Have you noticed that your child:	Yes	No
Seems to be quite clumsy and unco-ordinated?	☐	☐
Is late in deciding which hand to use for writing (after four and a half)?	☐	☐
Is finding it hard to use the correct pencil grip?	☐	☐
Does drawings that are little more than scribble even though she is four?	☐	☐
Is finding it hard to copy letters?	☐	☐
Doesn't want to pick up a pencil because it is 'too hard'?	☐	☐

If you have answered 'yes' to most of these questions, you might ask yourself, 'Could my child be dyspraxic?' Unfortunately, we know far less about dyspraxia than about dyslexia. Dyspraxia – or Developmental Co-ordination Difficulty (DCD) – describes children who are poorly co-ordinated and who may have difficulties with other 'non-verbal' skills. They may, for instance, be poor at picking out visual details or have problems with games like Lego, jigsaws and pencil-and-paper mazes.

Here are some tips if you are worried that your child might have dyspraxia or DCD:

- Do lots of drawing, painting, colouring in, tracing and stencilling, jigsaw puzzles, mazes, Lego, matching games and so on. These can help your child become more visually aware, as well as helping her fine motor skills.

- If you're still worried about your child's co-ordination, drawing or early writing skills as her first day at school gets closer, let school know. During the first term you and her teacher can keep a close eye on how these skills develop. It may be that your child is a little slower at drawing and writing than other skills like talking or reading – your child may 'take off' after a slow start, so be patient and give her time to make her own way.

- If she is still having problems after her first term, and is beginning to show signs of not wanting to write, it may be time to involve the school's Special Needs teacher. Some children have severe co-ordination problems, so may need to be assessed by a physiotherapist or occupational therapist.

★ **TOP TIP:** Have lots of fun with drawing and painting and colouring in – and look forward to the day when your child can sign her own artwork.

One Last Tip

The day will come when your child is actually off to school for the first time, or perhaps that time has come already.

Our biggest tip of all is to relax, see yourself as a 'good enough' parent and not feel you have to be perfect. You don't have to spend a huge amount of time and money to get your child prepared for school. Make the best use of the time you already have together to organise your routines and make life and learning easier. And use your play times together for having fun learning the skills needed for school. You will know that you have given your child the best chance of a happy and successful start at school.

Index

**Also available from Vermilion
by Dr Helen Likierman and Dr Valeire Muter...**

If you enjoyed this *Top Tips* edition, more comprehensive advice
and guidelines can be found in *Prepare Your Child for School*
(ISBN: 9780091906771, £8.99).

There is also comprehensive advice on dyslexia, dyspraxia and
other learning difficulties in *Dyslexia: A Parents' Guide to
Dyslexia, Dyspraxia and Other Learning Difficulties*
(ISBN: 9780091923389, £10.99).

FREE POSTAGE AND PACKING
Overseas customers allow £2.00 per paperback.

BY PHONE: 01624 677237

BY POST: Random House Books
c/o Bookpost, PO Box 29, Douglas
Isle of Man, IM99 1BQ

BY FAX: 01624 670923

BY EMAIL: bookshop@enterprise.net

Cheques (payable to Bookpost) and credit cards accepted.
Prices and availability subject to change without notice.
Allow 28 days for delivery.
When placing your order, please mention if you do not wish to receive any additional information.

www.rbooks.co.uk